"We all know fasting can be a spiritual exercise, but eating is really more like Jesus. In this book, Chester points out that Christianity was meant to be conducted at a table with the intimacy of a shared meal. Church was never meant to be holy services held in sacred buildings conducted by saintly men in long robes passing thin wafers and a thimble of juice—removed from real life. Chester rightly puts us back where we belong . . . at the table in front of a meal—a feast actually. This is an outstanding treatise on an important subject that was long ago lost in the mire of sacred rituals. It is time we come back to the table and enjoy the life given to us."

Neil Cole, founder and director,
Church Multiplication Associates; author, *Organic Church*

"I have always told the congregations I've served that if you take the mountains and meals out of the Bible, it's a very short book. In a world of competing church models and strategies, Tim shows us that Jesus employed one practice over all others: sharing a meal with people. This book serves as a poignant reminder that grace, mission, and community are never enacted best through programs and propaganda, but rather through the equality and acceptance experienced at the common table. May our lives never be too busy to live this out."

Mike Breen, Global Leader, 3DM;
author, *Building a Discipleship Culture*

"I'm not sure I could name all the titles of the books Tim has now written. I've even written one or two with him. But this is the best so far, by far! It fed my soul, and through it I enjoyed grace in a new way. In fact, the book is a sumptuous meal in its own right. Buy it, not just to read it, but to feast on it."

Steve Timmis, Executive Director,
Acts 29 Church Planting Network

"Tim Chester has a keen ability to reflect on gospel, community, and mission, making them accessible to the common person thr--- · 1ess and movement of everyday life. Tim c--- · 1 in *A Meal with Jesus*. With each mea   )el informs all of life and relationshi¡   or Jesus grew stronger. I want everyo

J

---rate;

.i~ionary Leader, Soma

A Meal with Jesus

A Meal WITH Jesus

Discovering Grace,
Community, & Mission
around the Table

TIM CHESTER

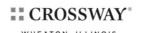

:: CROSSWAY®

WHEATON, ILLINOIS

A Meal with Jesus: Discovering Grace, Community, and Mission around the Table
Copyright © 2011 by Tim Chester
Published by Crossway
        1300 Crescent Street
        Wheaton, Illinois 60187

Interior design and typesetting: Lakeside Design Plus
Cover design: Patrick Mahoney
First printing 2011
Printed in the United States of America

Unless otherwise indicated, Scripture quotations are from the ESV® Bible (The Holy Bible, English Standard Version®), copyright © 2001 by Crossway. Used by permission. All rights reserved.

Scripture references marked NIV are from the HOLY BIBLE, NEW INTERNATIONAL VERSION®. Copyright © 1973, 1978, 1984 Biblica. Used by permission of Zondervan. All rights reserved. The "NIV" and "New International Version" trademarks are registered in the United States Patent and Trademark Office by Biblica. Use of either trademark requires the permission of Biblica.

All emphases in Scripture quotations have been added.

Trade Paperback ISBN: 978-1-4335-2136-2
PDF ISBN: 978-1-4335-2137-9
Mobipocket ISBN: 978-1-4335-2142-3
ePub ISBN: 978-1-4335-2143-0

Library of Congress Cataloging-in-Publication Data
Chester, Tim.
A meal with Jesus : discovering grace, community, and mission around the table / Tim Chester.
    p. cm.
  Includes bibliographical references (p.   ).
  ISBN 978-1-4335-2136-2 (tp)
  1. Mission of the church. 2. Dinners and dining—Religious aspects—Christianity. 3. Mission of the church—Biblical teaching. 4. Dinners and dining in the Bible. 5. Bible. N.T. Luke—Theology. I. Title.
BV601.8.C44 2011
262'.7—dc22   2010051422

Crossway is a publishing ministry of Good News Publishers.

Contents

Introduction

The Son of Man Came Eating and Drinking

I fell in love with my wife while she was making me cheese on toast. I'd only known her for a few weeks. It had been "love" at first sight for me, except of course that my initial "love" was mere attraction. No, it was the cheese on toast that won my heart. It wasn't that she could make cheese on toast—I was looking for a little more than that in a wife. But that simple act of service, done without thought to herself (plus her beautiful hands), captured my heart. My response at the time wasn't so reflective. I just knew she was the one for me.

I've now spent more than half my lifetime with the girl who once made me cheese on toast. Half a lifetime of shared meals. I still regard every meal she cooks as a gift. I think I've expressed my appreciation every time. It's not hard work. It's more an involuntary exclamation of delight than a disciplined duty. But it's not just the food. Each meal is an embodiment of her love for me. And for our two daughters. And our many guests. Her love doesn't consist merely in her cooking. But her cooking gives tangible—and edible—form to her love.

Food matters. Meals matter. Meals are full of significance. "Few acts are more expressive of companionship than the shared meal. . . . Someone with whom we share food is likely to be our friend, or well on the way to becoming one."[1] The word "companion" comes from the Latin "cum" ("together") and "panis" ("bread").

We all have favorite images of good hospitality. I think of my friends Andy and Josie and their farmhouse kitchen: vegetables fresh with garden mud, hot buns with a shiny glaze, warmth from the old stove, and the gentle flow of conversation from which talk of God is never absent for long. "Our life at the table, no matter how mundane, is sacramental—a means through which we encounter the mystery of God."[2]

Think about your dining room or kitchen table. What dramas have been played out around this simple piece of furniture? Day by day you've chatted with your family, sharing news, telling stories, and poking fun. Values have been imbibed. Guests have been welcomed. People have found a home. Love has blossomed. Perhaps you reached across the table to take the hand of your beloved for the first time. Perhaps you remember important decisions made round the table. Perhaps you were reconciled with another over a meal. Perhaps your family still bonds by laughing at the time you forgot to add sugar to your cake.

In my favorite food writer's autobiography, Nigel Slater describes how as a boy he once said his mother's kisses were like marshmallows. When Slater was nine, his mother died, and his father started leaving marshmallows beside his bed each night.[3]

Food connects. It connects us with family. It turns strangers into friends. And it connects us with people around the world. Consider what you had for breakfast this morning. Tea. Coffee. Sugar. Cereal. Grapefruit. Much of it was produced in another state or country. Food enables us to be blessed by people around the world and to bless them in return.

But hospitality can also have its dark side. I once attended a meeting at the World Bank offices in London. Offered coffee (one of the few things I don't like), I asked if there was tea. "We don't serve tea in the morning," I was told in a tone dripping with condescension. I had well and truly been put in my place. People like me were not welcome. But this is a trivial example compared to the race and class prejudices expressed through hospitality or its absence. Nothing bespoke the way the world stood before the civil rights movement more than the "no blacks" signs on restaurant doors. Or the "no blacks, no Irish, no dogs" signs outside lodgings in the UK. Hospitality was just as important in the ancient world. New Testament scholar John Koenig says: "When guests or hosts violate their obligations to each other, the whole world shakes and retribution follows."[4]

The global connections of trade also have their dark side, as the powerful use their power to exploit the weak. In the eighteenth and nineteenth centuries it was sugar and slavery. Today exploitation can be found amidst migrant laborers, subsistence farmers undercut by the dumping of subsidized exports, and workers in food processing plants in economic development zones exempt from labor laws. "An unplowed field produces food for the poor, but injustice sweeps it away" (Prov. 13:23, NIV). The food we purchase enables us to bless others—or curse them.

Our relationship to food is ambiguous. Television chefs have become celebrities, and cookbooks regularly appear on bestseller lists. Yet we cook less than ever before. Americans spend over $50 billion on dieting each year—$50 billion to solve the problem of food gone wrong. At any given moment 25 percent of American men and 45 percent of women are dieting. Only 9 percent of college-aged women have never tried to control their weight through dieting. American Christians spend more on dieting than on world missions.[5] We spend more curing our overconsumption than we do feeding the physically and spiritually hungry of the world. We express who we want to be through food. And when things go wrong, food becomes a place of refuge. The brokenhearted console themselves on the sofa with a tub of ice cream. You are what you eat, people say. Food is so much more than fuel.

How would you complete the sentence: "The Son of Man came . . ."? The Son of Man came . . . preaching the Word . . . to establish the kingdom of God . . . to die on the cross.

Perhaps the question is more revealing if we make it, "We should go . . ."? We should go . . . campaign for political change . . . preach on street corners . . . make the most of new media . . . adapt to the culture we want to reach.

There are three ways the New Testament completes the sentence, "The Son of Man came . . ." "The Son of Man came not to be served but to serve, and to give his life as a ransom for many" (Mark 10:45); "The Son of Man came to seek and to save the lost" (Luke 19:10); "The Son of Man has come eating and drinking . . ." (Luke 7:34).

The first two are statements of purpose. *Why* did Jesus come? He came to serve, to give his life as a ransom, to seek and save the lost. The third is a statement of method. *How* did Jesus come? He came eating and drinking.

"Son of Man" is Daniel's label for one who comes before God to receive authority over the nations (Daniel 7). And now Jesus, the Son of Man, has come. But how does he come? Does he come with an army of angels? Does he come on the clouds of heaven? Does he come with a blaze of glory? No, he comes "eating and drinking."

The Jews of Jesus's day would have said the Son of Man will come to vindicate the righteous and defeat God's enemies. They didn't expect him to come to seek and save the lost. And they would have said the Son of Man will come in glory and power. They would never have said he would come eating and drinking.

And Luke is not talking about just subsistence eating and drinking. Jesus says: "The Son of Man has come eating and drinking, and you say, 'Look at him! A glutton and a drunkard, a friend of tax collectors and sinners!'" (7:34). A glutton, of course, is someone who eats too much, and a drunkard is someone who drinks too much. Jesus was seriously into eating and drinking—so much so that his enemies accused him of doing it to excess. Earlier in Luke's Gospel the Pharisees and their scribes said to him, "The disciples of John fast often and offer prayers, and so do the disciples of the Pharisees, but yours eat and drink" (5:33). Jesus spent his time eating and drinking—a lot of his time. He was a party animal. His mission strategy was a long meal, stretching into the evening. He did evangelism and discipleship round a table with some grilled fish, a loaf of bread, and a pitcher of wine.

Luke's Gospel is full of stories of Jesus eating with people:

- In Luke 5 Jesus eats with tax collectors and sinners at the home of Levi.
- In Luke 7 Jesus is anointed at the home of Simon the Pharisee during a meal.
- In Luke 9 Jesus feeds the five thousand.
- In Luke 10 Jesus eats in the home of Martha and Mary.
- In Luke 11 Jesus condemns the Pharisees and teachers of the law at a meal.
- In Luke 14 Jesus is at a meal when he urges people to invite the poor to their meals rather than their friends.
- In Luke 19 Jesus invites himself to dinner with Zacchaeus.
- In Luke 22 we have the account of the Last Supper.
- In Luke 24 the risen Christ has a meal with the two disciples in Emmaus, and then later eats fish with the disciples in Jerusalem.

Robert Karris concludes: "In Luke's Gospel Jesus is either going to a meal, at a meal, or coming from a meal."[6]

Even when Jesus is not eating, references to food abound throughout the Gospel. In Luke 14 Jesus tells a parable of a great banquet. In Luke 15 Jesus tells the parable of the prodigal son, which ends with a party. In Luke 16 he contrasts a rich man "who feasted sumptuously every day" (v. 19) with a beggar "who desired to be fed with what fell from the rich man's table." Luke tells about the women who provided food for Jesus (8:2–3). When asked if few are saved, Jesus warns people to ensure they themselves enter the kingdom, for on the last day people will say, "we ate and drank in your presence. . . ." But "the master of the house" will say, "I do not know where you come from. Depart from me. . . ." Instead, "people will come from east and west, and from north and south, and recline at table in the kingdom of God" (see Luke 13:22–30). In Luke 22 Jesus tells his disciples: "I assign to you, as my Father assigned to me, a kingdom, that you may eat and drink at my table in my kingdom . . ." (vv. 29–30). Food is used to describe salvation and judgment (1:53; 6:21, 25), and people are described in terms of good food and bad food (3:17; 6:43–46; 12:1).

Jesus is called "a glutton and a drunkard, a friend of tax collectors and sinners." This is why eating and drinking were so important in the mission of Jesus: they were a sign of his friendship with tax collectors and sinners. His "excess" of food and "excess" of grace are linked. In the ministry of Jesus, meals were enacted grace, community, and mission.

So the meals of Jesus represent something bigger. They represent a new world, a new kingdom, a new outlook. But they give that new reality substance. Jesus's meals are not just symbols; they're also application. They're not just pictures; they're the real thing in miniature. Food is stuff. It's not ideas. It's not theories. It's, well, it's food, and you put it in your mouth, taste it, and eat it. And meals are more than food. They're social occasions. They represent friendship, community, and welcome.

I don't want to reduce church and mission to meals, but I do want to argue that meals should be an integral and significant part of our shared life. They represent the meaning of mission, but they more than represent it: they embody and enact our mission. Community and mission are more than meals, but it's hard to conceive of them without meals. Peter Leithart says:

> For Jesus "feast" was not just a "metaphor" for the kingdom. As Jesus announced the feast of the kingdom, He also brought it into reality through His own feasting. Unlike may theologians, He did not come preaching an ideology, promoting ideas, or teaching moral maxims. He came teaching about the feast of the kingdom, and He came feasting in the kingdom. Jesus did not go around merely talking about eating and drinking; he went around eating and drinking. A lot.[7]

This is a book about meals. But the meals of Jesus are a window into his message of grace and the way it defines his community and its mission. So this book is about grace, church, and mission. But meals are more than metaphor. They embody God's grace and so give form to community and mission. We can't get away from meals.

If I pull down books on mission and church planting from my shelves, I can read about contextualization, evangelism matrices, postmodern apologetics, and cultural hermeneutics. I can look at diagrams that tell me how people can be converted or discover the steps required to plant a church. It all sounds impressive, cutting edge, and sophisticated. But this is how Luke describes Jesus's mission strategy: "The Son of Man came eating and drinking."

We can make community and mission sound like specialized activities that belong to experts. Some people have a vested interest in doing this, because it makes them feel "extraordinary." Or we focus on dynamic personalities who can hold an audience and lead a movement. Some push mission beyond the scope of "ordinary" Christians. But the Son of Man came eating and drinking. It's not complicated. True, it's not always easy—it involves people invading your space or going to places where you don't feel comfortable. But it's not complicated. If you share a meal three or four times a week and you have a passion for Jesus, then you will be building up the Christian community and reaching out in mission.

Let's see how Jesus did it.

1

Meals as Enacted Grace

Luke 5

It was midnight, and I was sitting down to the biggest plate of meat I'd ever attempted to consume. Unfortunately, I'd just eaten the equivalent of a full meal.

I'd spent the day with Daniel and Marie Elena Ruffinatti, who work in Argentina with prisoners and people in psychiatric institutions, as well as their families.

On my first day with the Ruffinattis we visited the largest psychiatric hospital in Argentina, which had over 1,300 men living in large, plain wards with nothing to do. The first man we met had been in the institution since he was eight. He was now in his midfifties. Most had received little love throughout their lives. They had usually been abandoned by their families, and the director conceded that most of his staff didn't really care for the patients. But Daniel and Marie Elena greeted everyone with great affection, and people's faces lit up when they saw them.

We then went to Daniel and Marie Elena's home, where we met Nico, their eight-year-old adopted son who had been abandoned by one of the prisoners. Nico had HIV. He spoke no English and I spoke no Spanish, but he proudly showed me his magnificent tree house. Daniel

17

told me he'd built it in style to teach Nico that God was preparing a home for him when he died.

By 5:30 p.m. I was ready for a quiet evening and an early night. But instead we headed off again into the city to a high-security jail to visit prisoners who were dying of AIDS. It was a horrible place. The smell was awful and the people were in a terrible state—weak, bedridden, dying. Yet Daniel and Maria Elena embraced these people, bringing sweets and shampoo, praying with them, and showing love.

We finally left the jail at 10:30 p.m. This is what Daniel and Marie Elena do week in, week out. We hadn't eaten, so we went to a restaurant. Argentineans eat lots of meat. I thought the salads served as a starter were the main meal because they included so much meat. After working my way through a plate of meat and salad, I was presented with the main course. And so it was that at midnight I faced two cuts of meat, either of which would have equaled a family Sunday roast. Daniel and Marie Elena's story demonstrates the radical power of God's grace, grace that Jesus embodied in his meals.

Luke 5:27–32

After this he went out and saw a tax collector named Levi, sitting at the tax booth. And he said to him, "Follow me." And leaving everything, he rose and followed him.

And Levi made him a great feast in his house, and there was a large company of tax collectors and others reclining at table with them. And the Pharisees and their scribes grumbled at his disciples, saying, "Why do you eat and drink with tax collectors and sinners?" And Jesus answered them, "Those who are well have no need of a physician, but those who are sick. I have not come to call the righteous but sinners to repentance."

The problem here is not the party. The Pharisees knew God's kingdom was going to be a party. Their objection is with the guest list.

Tax collectors were social outcasts who commonly used their position to cheat people. But there is more to their story. They were collaborators. They were working for the enemy. But there's more to it even than that. The Jews were looking for the day when God would defeat the Romans and re-establish his kingdom. So it wasn't just Jews versus Romans, it was God versus Romans. And the tax collectors had opted for the Romans. They were traitors to the nation *and* they were traitors to God. They were God's enemies.

And here they are partying with God's Messiah. God is sitting down and eating with his enemies.

To see how scandalous this is we need to appreciate the role meals played in the culture of the day. New Testament scholar Scott Bartchy says:

> It would be difficult to overestimate the importance of table fellowship for the cultures of the Mediterranean basin in the first century of our era. Mealtimes were far more than occasions for individuals to consume nourishment. Being welcomed at a table for the purpose of eating food with another person had become a ceremony richly symbolic of friendship, intimacy and unity. Thus betrayal or unfaithfulness toward anyone with whom one had shared the table was viewed as particularly reprehensible. On the other hand, when persons were estranged, a meal invitation opened the way to reconciliation.[1]

In a famous essay, anthropologist Mary Douglas showed that in all cultures meals represent "boundary markers." They mark the boundaries between different levels of intimacy and acceptance.[2] Douglas also outlined an influential analysis of the laws in Leviticus about food and sexual purity. She argued that they weren't primitive health regulations, but they concerned boundary maintenance. "It would seem that whenever a people are aware of encroachment and danger, dietary rules controlling what goes into the body would serve as a vivid analogy of the corpus of their cultural categories at risk."[3] Policing the human body was a way of policing the social body by maintaining a common identity.

Jewish food laws not only symbolized cultural boundaries, they also created them. It wasn't easy for Jews to eat with Gentiles—it still isn't today. You couldn't be sure you were being offered kosher food prepared in a kosher way (different utensils had to be used for meat and dairy, the blood had to be properly drained, and so on). If followed faithfully, dietary regulations inevitably meant Israelites couldn't enter into the intimate relationships that shared meals create. Scholars believe that Jews rarely ate with Gentiles in Jesus's day.[4] When Isaiah promised a great banquet, it included "all peoples," "all nations," "all faces," and "all the earth" (Isa. 25:6–8). But in the years before Jesus, the Gentiles had dropped off the guest list in Jewish hopes for the coming banquet.[5]

By the time we get to first-century Judaism, dietary laws had become still more detailed and created even stronger boundaries—within Judaism as well as outside. The wound at the heart of Judaism was Gentile occupation of the Promised Land. The Pharisees believed Israel had to be pure before she could be restored. Pharisaism was a lay movement that, while not completely rejecting the temple system, sought to extend its purity laws into one's own home. So they exhorted all Jews to observe voluntarily the purity code that the Torah required only of priests—and to do so all year round. "The Pharisees regarded their tables at home as surrogates for the Lord's altar in the Temple in Jerusalem and therefore strove to maintain in their households and among their eating companions the state of ritual purity required of priests in Temple service. . . . The Pharisees longed for the time when all of Israel would live in such a state of holiness. They believed that Israel's identity and blessed future depended on it."[6]

Luke describes Jesus's table companions as "tax collectors and *others*" (5:29). It's the Pharisees who call them "tax collectors and *sinners*" (v. 30). The message is clear: these "others" don't measure up to the standards of purity expected by the Pharisees.

Even these standards weren't enough for another Jewish sect, the Essenes. The Essenes inhabited the Qumran community where the Dead Sea Scrolls were found. They felt the nation was so contaminated that the only way forward was to live as an isolated community in the desert.

A central question in the Judaism of Jesus's day was: With whom can I eat? Present holiness and future expectation were bound up in this question. "Doing lunch was doing theology."[7] Jesus doesn't so much provide a new answer to the question as completely undermine its premise. He renders the question irrelevant.

Inclusion was the issue at another meal Jesus attended.

Luke 11:37–41

While Jesus was speaking, a Pharisee asked him to dine with him, so he went in and reclined at table. The Pharisee was astonished to see that he did not first wash before dinner. And the Lord said to him, "Now you Pharisees cleanse the outside of the cup and of the dish, but inside you are full of greed and wickedness. You fools! Did not he who made the outside make the inside also? But give as alms those things that are within, and behold, everything is clean for you."

Jesus doesn't wash before the meal. It's a provocative act. It's the cultural equivalent of refusing a handshake. Then, before anything else is said, Jesus says, "You're full of greed, you fools." That's rude in any culture! This isn't Jesus meek and mild. This is Jesus spoiling for a fight. The Pharisees' system of ritual cleanliness stinks, Jesus says. These religious leaders are like cups that are rinsed on the outside, but inside are the molding remains of coffee dregs and lipstick. Jesus finds it repulsive. "This cup may look clean on the outside," Jesus says in effect, "but if you really want it to be clean, use it to offer aid to the poor."

As far as the Pharisees were concerned, if you gave a dish to the poor it became unclean, because the poor were the great unwashed who didn't fulfill ceremonial washing. But Jesus says the dish becomes clean because it expresses love. The cleanliness that counts is found in the heart (Mark 7:20–23).

But Jesus's critique of these outwardly respectable people goes further. The Pharisees may look respectable, but Jesus calls them "unmarked graves" (Luke 11:44). Though people don't see it, they're dead inside.

The reference to the poor is significant. When a teacher of the law intervenes, Jesus replies, "Woe to you lawyers also! For you load people with burdens hard to bear, and you yourselves do not touch the burdens with one of your fingers" (Luke 11:46). The effect of this ritual cleansing was not only to create boundaries with Gentiles, but also with the poor. The religious elite had created a system of moral respectability that only the wealthy could ever hope to maintain. Only the rich had the time and money to do all the required ritual cleansing. You can't be ritually clean in a slum. This was bourgeois spirituality. We can do this too. Our expectations of clothing, behavior, literacy, and punctuality can exclude the poor. These verses also speak to a professionalized church ministry—a life seen as the epitome of godliness, but all but impossible for those not in full-time ministry.

The teachers of the law created a system that allowed them to feel superior, and then lifted not one finger to help others. Think how this might play out today. Today's Pharisees might condemn the poor for their dysfunctional families, but lift not one finger to help. Today's Pharisees might condemn the poor for their excessive drinking, but lift not one finger to ease their pain. Today's Pharisees might condemn the poor for their laziness, but lift not one finger to provide employment. Today's Pharisees might condemn the poor for their abortions, but lift not one finger to adopt unwanted children. I'm not defending dysfunctional families, drunkenness, and so on. But we can't condemn these things at a distance. That's legalism. We must come alongside, proclaiming and demonstrating the transforming grace of God.

The Pharisees are people who have the Word, but hide it. Formally they honor the Word, building monuments for the prophets. But in reality they ignore God's Word, effectively siding with those who killed the prophets (Luke 11:47–51). They'd created a system that the poor could never keep, and then instead of helping them, despised them for their failures. Jesus concludes: "Woe to you lawyers! For you have taken away the key of knowledge. You did not enter yourselves, and you hindered those who were entering" (11:52).

How might we do this today? Perhaps through sophisticated displays of exegesis or rhetoric that make the nonliterate feel that they can't read the Bible for themselves. Perhaps through application that focuses on externals and leaves hearts unchanged. Perhaps by applying the text to dodgy charismatics or Catholics or dispensationalists or fundamentalists or liberals or pagans—anyone but ourselves. Perhaps by reading the Bible through theological grids so we say what the text does *not* say rather than what it does say. Perhaps by emphasizing knowledge but not obedience or love. A key theme in Luke's Gospel is "heeding" the Word of God. "Heeding" is an old word, but one that beautifully combines both *hearing* and *doing*.

Jesus is handing out God's party invitations. They read: "*You're invited to my party in the new creation. Come as you are.*" The religious leaders agreed there was a party and an invitation and even that it was possible to attend. But when the religious leaders passed out the invitation, they didn't say, "Come as you are." They said, "You've got to get changed; you've got to get cleaned up." As a result people didn't come, because they didn't think they were good enough. This is how the Pharisees took away the key of knowledge.

It's been a great privilege for me to know Saul and Pilar Cruz, and to participate in their ministry to the slums of Mexico City. Saul was brought up in a good and proper evangelical church. Pilar was converted through a Bible study he was leading, and soon they started dating. Saul's mother disapproved. Pilar to this day wears high heels and short skirts—this is not how a good, middle-class, evangelical

Christian is supposed to dress. Saul's mother noticed that Pilar had stopped attending church in the morning. Her suspicions about her son's girlfriend were confirmed. So one Sunday Saul secretly followed Pilar. She took a bus across town to a poor neighborhood, where she met an older man, and together they held an impromptu Sunday school on the pavement for slum children. After a while Pilar came over to where Saul (who thought he was hiding) was and told him he may as well join in. Her explanation for her absence from church? "If Jesus is Savior, then he's the Savior of these people as well, and your church is doing nothing to reach them." Saul told me with a twinkle in his eye, "That's when I knew for sure she was the woman for me."

They began working with a local church in a poor neighborhood. The church members were more affluent and came from outside the area. Saul and Pilar began reaching prostitutes and drug addicts, befriending them, serving their needs, and sharing the gospel with them. Some of them started coming to church. Then one Sunday morning they turned up to find the building locked. The members of the church didn't want prostitutes and drug addicts corrupting their children, so without any consultation they'd decided to move elsewhere. The culture gap between the church and the marginalized had proved too big for the church members.

So Saul and Pilar started again. Someone gave them a garbage dump in a slum area on which they built an "urban transformation center" called Armonia. They didn't call it a church because of the negative connotations people from the slums had for that word.

At one point they created a housing project. But when they came to hand over the new homes, they realized couples weren't properly married. It was simply too expensive for the poor to marry because of the certificates required and the cultural expectations of a lavish party. This meant the women had no legal protection.

The teachers of the law in Luke 11 would have wagged their fingers. Saul and Pilar lifted their fingers to help. They started organizing community weddings. They married ten or so couples at a time in the community center. They pulled some favors with a local judge to preside over the ceremony for free, persuaded wealthy churches to buy rings, and threw a banquet for all the community. On one occasion one man got married at the same ceremony as his grandparents.

Grace Turns Everything Upside Down

Come back with me to Levi's party. Please have some sympathy for the Pharisees. Jesus welcomes the enemies of God. Surely this makes any claims that Jesus might be from God nonsense. Can you see how their position makes good sense?

Unless . . . Unless God is doing something new—so new it doesn't fit any of the old categories. Unless God is doing something so gracious it takes us completely by surprise.

Look at what is happening around this meal in Luke 5.

In Luke 5:12–15 Jesus touches a leper. Normally if you did that, you became unclean. But instead of Jesus becoming unclean, the leper becomes clean. This is God's grace in action. God's grace welcomes the outcast and brings transformation. Suddenly it isn't uncleanness that's contagious. That's how it was in the old Levitical system. If you touched anything unclean, you became unclean. But with Jesus it's his holiness that's contagious.

Jesus isn't rejecting the purity laws of Leviticus because they were wrong; he's showing that they're being fulfilled. Leviticus pointed to the need for a holy people; Jesus is the one who will atone for sin, baptize with the Holy Spirit, and write God's law on our hearts. Levitical-style cleanliness is being superseded.

In Luke 5:17–26 Jesus not only heals a paralyzed man, he forgives his sin. Forgiveness of sin at that time was focused on the rituals of the temple. But Jesus forgives with just a word, without reference to the temple. What the temple symbolized is giving way to the reality to which it pointed.

In Luke 5:33–35 the Pharisees ask why Jesus's disciples don't fast. The Jews fasted to call upon God to come in mercy to liberate the nation. But what if God's Messiah, full of mercy, is here, sitting at the table with the tax collectors?

In Luke 5:36–39 Jesus makes the point explicitly. Something new is happening—something so new it can't be added onto the old, any more than you can sew new cloth on old. This is not simply an amendment to the old system. Grace can't be integrated with self-righteousness and self-importance. It's radically different, radically new.

The parties of Jesus are celebrations. The Pharisees are mourning over the absence of God and his kingdom. But in Jesus God has come to his people, and his kingdom is dawning. So fasting gives way to feasting. Their meals are eaten with joy. They must be.

Compare the old way with the new way. The new way is gracious rather than religious, inclusive rather than exclusive, welcoming rather than unwelcoming. It is characterized by feasting rather than fasting, rejoicing rather than grumbling. It recognizes its need and finds hope in the Savior rather than feeling self-righteous and therefore rejecting the Savior.

Look at those two lists: gracious, inclusive, welcoming, feasting, rejoicing, and recognizing your need, compared with religious, exclusive, unwelcoming, fasting, grumbling, and self-righteous. Are you living as someone who belongs to the new way?

This is how Jesus explains himself: "Those who are well have no need of a physician, but those who are sick. I have not come to call the righteous but sinners to repentance" (Luke 5:31–32). The Pharisees are asking Jesus to behave like a doctor who avoids sick people. Such a doctor clearly couldn't do his work. Jesus the Savior can't do his work unless he's with sinful people.

It's the same for those who follow Jesus. We can't do our work of pointing sinners to the Savior unless we spend time with them. The first thing Levi does after following Jesus is to throw a party.

Maybe like Levi you introduced Jesus to your friends when you first became a Christian. But after a while you lost contact with those friends. Perhaps the church schedule left little time. Perhaps your new behavior made it hard to hang out with old friends. Perhaps you were warned of the influence they might have on you. But those who avoid the contamination of sinners are like the Pharisees. Those who earn the label "friend of sinners" are like their Savior.

*

The grace of God is radically subversive. Running through Luke's Gospel is the message that the last day will involve a radical reversal in which the first shall be last and the last shall be first. The meals of Jesus picture that day, as he welcomes the marginal and confronts the self-righteous and self-reliant.

Grace turns the world of religious people upside down. They think of life as a ladder. Your righteous acts move you up the ladder toward God. Your sense of well-being comes from your place on the ladder. Nothing makes you feel better than being able to look down on other people. Pharisees need tax collectors to make them feel righteous.

But the grace of God is also radically subversive of the secular counterparts. Everyone is trying to find salvation. They might not ask, "What must I do to be saved?" But everyone has some sense of what it is that would make them satisfied, fulfilled, and accepted: success in business, the admiration of men, a beautiful home, a liberated homeland, a secure future, the worship of women, a great body, wealth and prosperity, the acceptance of friends, a happy family, a dream vacation.

Think about the people you know. Think about yourself.

1. How do they define salvation? How will they know they've arrived? *"I'll be happy, fulfilled, accepted if . . ."*

27

2. What must they do to be saved? What law or rules must they follow? *"To achieve this I've got to . . ."*
3. How do they view people who don't measure up to this law? *"People who don't fit in are . . ."*
4. What happens when they don't measure up? *"When I don't achieve, then . . ."*

For the Pharisees it went like this: Salvation is national renewal. This will be achieved by personal purity. Those who don't measure up, like tax collectors, sinners, and the poor, must be ostracized.

Every version of salvation involves a principle, a rule, a law. If your idea of salvation is to have friends accept you, then your first commandment will be: "Thou shalt not be uncool." And uncool people must be avoided at all costs. If your idea of salvation is a beautiful home, then your prophet will be Martha Stewart. Your rule will be antique pine, tiled floors, and distressed paint. Or maybe clean lines, white walls, and no clutter. Your first commandment will be: "Thou shalt not be untidy."

If other people don't measure up, then we despise or avoid them. Yet, like the Pharisees, we need them so we can feel good about ourselves. And if we don't measure up, then our "god" turns on us and condemns us. Life is seen as a race, and you're a loser if you're not successful, wealthy, or attractive.

But self-salvation doesn't work. It doesn't work, because none of these versions of salvation deliver. They don't bring satisfaction, identity, or joy, because we were made to know God and glorify him. Anything less is a cheap substitute. They're not salvation!

And self-salvation doesn't work because we can't measure up. If you want to be admired by blokes, but you're not blokey enough, then you're condemned. Even on a good day you'll worry what others think of you. If you want security and prosperity, and you lose your job, then you're condemned. Even when you have a job, you'll be anxious, over-busy, and unable to say no. "We know that a person is not justified by works of the law but through faith in Jesus Christ . . ." (Gal. 2:16).

The good news is that Jesus has not come "to call the righteous but sinners to repentance."

He offers true salvation: being welcomed to God's feast. And when we don't measure up, we're not condemned. Instead of condemning us, our God is condemned in our place. So salvation is found not through obeying any kind of law, but "through faith in Jesus."

No One Gets Left Behind

The film *Little Miss Sunshine* is the story of a girl who by default gets through to the regional final of the Little Miss Sunshine beauty contest. Her dysfunctional family heads off for the pageant. Olive is an awkward girl with big glasses about to enter a beauty contest. At one point she says, "I don't want to be a loser, because Daddy hates losers." Her father is a failed motivational speaker. His conversation consists of clichéd aphorisms that berate people for being losers. The irony, of course, is that he's a loser and his family are losers. At one points he says, "There are two kinds of people in this world: winners and losers." On the word "losers" the camera pans around his family: his foul-mouthed father, his suicidal, homosexual brother-in-law, his son who refuses to speak, his downtrodden wife desperately trying to hold them all together, and himself, the failed businessman who can't face his failure. And they're thrown together in a VW van, which is itself dysfunctional: the door falls off, the horn is constantly on, and they must push-start it every time. I sometimes look around my congregation and see a bunch of dysfunctional people thrown together, somehow managing to be family. And I smile at the ridiculous grace of God.

There's a moment in the film when the family suddenly realizes that Olive isn't in the van. They've left her behind at the gas station. We see the van moving across the screen in one direction, and they collect her—without stopping, because they can't restart the van. Then we see the van moving back across in the other direction, and we hear the father's voice: "No one gets left behind, no one gets left behind." That's the church: the place where no one gets left behind.

At the film's climax this dysfunctional family arrives at the beauty contest. It's the epitome of a perfect, respectable, manicured (literally) world without blemish or fault, but there is a seething undertone of envy, rivalry, and arrogance. And these two worlds collide with comic results. That's what's going on at Levi's party: two worlds are colliding. Jesus comes crashing into the Pharisees' world of self-reliance, pride, superiority, hypocrisy, and self-justification with his utterly subversive message of God's grace.

Levi's party and the stories describing the new, gracious thing God is doing come to a climax in Luke 6:11: "[The scribes and Pharisees] were filled with fury and discussed with one another what they might do to Jesus." Robert Karris says: "In Luke's Gospel Jesus got himself killed because of the way he ate."[8] When Jesus eats with Levi, the message is clear: Jesus has come for losers, people on the margins, people who've made a mess of their lives, people who are ordinary. Jesus has come for you. The only people left out are those who think they don't need God: the self-righteous and the self-important. Sadly that includes many people.

Three Stories of Grace

Luke 15 contains three famous parables: the lost sheep, the lost coin, and the lost son. But notice why these parables were told: "Now the tax collectors and sinners were all drawing near to hear him. And the Pharisees and the scribes grumbled, saying, 'This man receives sinners and eats with them'" (vv. 1–2).

It's the same issue we met at Levi's house. There's something about Jesus that makes tax collectors and sinners want to be with him. And Jesus eats with them—a sign of friendship and fellowship. But the Pharisees and the teachers of the law are scandalized. So Jesus tells these three parables to explain himself. In a sense they expand his statement in Luke 5:31–32 that he has come for sinners, not for the righteous. He's come for those who are lost, and when the lost are found, there's always a party. The shepherd, the woman, and the father each hold a party (15:6, 9, 23–24) that mirrors the celebration of heaven (15:7, 10).

All three parables speak of the sinners and tax collectors—they're like the lost sheep, the lost coin, and the lost son that Jesus has come to find and rescue. I recently read the parable of the prodigal with a young woman struggling with anorexia. We both marveled at how the story spoke so directly to her. I've read it hundreds of times, but it was only through reading it with her that I realized how integral food is to the story. I knew food represented the height of the younger son's recovery. But food also represents the depths of his lostness. We know how lost he is when he longs to share a meal with pigs. It's then he remembers that his father's servants "have more than enough bread," while away from his father "I perish here with hunger" (Luke 15:17).

But the third parable also speaks of the Pharisees. They're like the older brother. The older brother is angry because the welcome of the prodigal makes his work seem meaningless. He worked hard for a reward, and now the younger son gets a reward without working. That's the scandal of grace. It means that if you've been working hard to be right with God, then you've been wasting your time because God welcomes everyone—righteous and unrighteous alike. God has no discrimination. It's too much for the older brother, and he refuses to join the party.

So his father goes out to him. There's grace for the younger son, but there's also grace for the older brother. Jesus himself eats with tax collectors and sinners, but he also eats with Pharisees (Luke 7, 11, 14). Jesus "is not self-righteous about self-righteousness."[9] The older brother is missing the party because he won't let go of the claims he thinks he has on his father. The story ends unresolved. Will he go in or not? We don't know. We're left asking the question. And as we ask it of the older brother, we inevitably ask it of ourselves. Would I have gone in? How do I feel about God's extravagant grace?

In Levi's party and the parables of Luke 15, salvation comes to the margins of society. That's good news to people at the margins today—and to everyone else. But if we reject salvation at the margins, if we reject those whom God accepts, then we reject the grace of God. We miss out on the celebration.

As we look further at the meals of Jesus in Luke's Gospel, we will discover:

- how God graciously includes those the world excludes;
- God's promise of an eternal banquet in a new creation;
- how we reflect God's welcome of us in the way we welcome others;
- how Jesus opens up the banquet through his death and resurrection;
- how the gracious invitation of God comes to us in the Word of God;
- how meals express grace, community, and mission.

For now let's marvel at just how gracious God is. In Jesus God is doing something so new and so gracious that it takes us by surprise. Indeed, it's so gracious it scandalizes us. God is indiscriminate. He chooses all the wrong sorts of people. He invites everyone to his great party. He invites the best and the worst, the highest and lowest. He invites you.

*

At midnight, as I worked my way through that plate of meat, Daniel told me his story, a story of the transforming power of grace. He came from a Christian family. As a teenager he lived what he called "a hypocritical double life." Outwardly respectable. A member of the church choir. But when he got a girl pregnant, they ran away together.

He joined the police hoping for a cushy desk job. But this was during military rule, and the training was a form of brainwashing. The trainees were taught to break into cars, cope with tear gas, and fight blindfolded. They were also indoctrinated, learning to hate Jews and terrorists. After six months Daniel was selected for an elite antiterrorist corp. He told of guarding a door behind which people were being tortured. Another time they "processed" a truck with thirty "packages"—a euphemism for men being taken away to be killed. He started losing control, becoming violent. He attacked his family and other officers, including superiors. He got involved in criminal activities. He did his first armed robbery with a hand grenade that he still owns.

Eventually Daniel was arrested for charges that included killing a police corporal. He wasn't tried in a criminal court because he was considered insane; he was put instead in a secure mental institution. For two years he lived in a bare cell with no toilet and no clothes except a straightjacket, taking a daily cocktail of forty drugs.

At one point he shared a cell with someone who believed God didn't exist, but that the Devil did. This man suggested they read the Bible in forty days so he could find out about Satan. Daniel was reluctant, but the other man couldn't read because his drugs had affected his eyes. So Daniel started reading fifty-nine pages a day, the rate required to complete the Bible in forty days. On day four he read: "The word is very near you. It is in your mouth and in your heart, so that you can do it. . . . I call heaven and earth to witness against you today that I have set before you life and death, blessing and curse. Therefore choose life, that you and your offspring may live" (Deut. 30:14, 19). Both men felt God powerfully with them at that moment. The other man didn't want to continue, but Daniel continued reading alone. After a few days he asked God to release him. Immediately he was free from tobacco and his cocktail of drugs, and he was in his right mind. Within two years he was released to do a menial job in the hospital, and then a few months later he was allowed to leave.

God's grace in Daniel's life radically changed him, making him a gracious person who has committed his life to the marginalized. The day after our meal we had a picnic for about fifty patients from the psychiatric hospital. We drank "mate" (a traditional Argentine drink), played soccer, talked, and sat in the sun. The patients could have a shower, a haircut, and a change of clothes. At the end of the afternoon we all gathered together. We sang Christian songs. Those with birthdays came to the front, and we sang "Happy Birthday." Just like the meals of Jesus, the picnic beautifully embodied God's love for this marginalized people. It spoke powerfully of grace, even to those among them who could not understand what was being said.

Daniel read the story of the prodigal son and told them three things. First, we have a good Father. Daniel asked the patients how we know God is good. Someone said, "God gave us this day," and Daniel said, "Yes, which businessman can give you a new morning?" Second, we have all turned from God like the son in the story, rejecting his love and living for ourselves. Third, God is ready to embrace us. In one sense we're far from God. But in another sense God is very close to us—just as he was for Daniel in his psychiatric cell.

In the story the son "came to his senses" (15:17, NIV). He doesn't go back saying, "I've a right to be treated like your son." He knows he's thrown away his rights. Instead he says, "I have no rights. But please forgive me. I'm a mess. Please let me be your servant." But here's the amazing thing. The father doesn't listen. He embraces him as a son. The son only gets halfway through his prepared speech when the father starts arranging a party to celebrate his return. Fathers in Jesus's day never ran—it was beneath their dignity. But God runs to meet us.

There were two women in the first cell we entered when we visited the prisoners dying from AIDS. One was Sonia, a former prostitute. She said she wanted to believe, but found it hard. So Daniel spoke to her of the father in the story, the Father who was ready to embrace her. The other woman, Sonilda, took her Bible from under her pillow and said she was sure God accepted her. She read from one of the psalms:

> In you, O LORD, do I take refuge;
>   let me never be put to shame!
> In your righteousness deliver me and rescue me;
>   incline your ear to me, and save me!
> Be to me a rock of refuge,
>   to which I may continually come;
> you have given the command to save me,
>   for you are my rock and my fortress. (Ps. 71:1–3)

This is how great God's grace is. Grace reaches down from heaven into a high-security prison in Argentina to a woman who's committed serious crimes, a woman dying of AIDS, a woman separated from her family, and says, "God is your rock of refuge."

God's grace reaches down from heaven into a mental institution to a man who's committed terrible crimes, who's out of his mind, and who's reached the depths of human existence and transforms his life, making him a courageous, loving, and whole person.

And God's grace can reach down to you.

2

Meals as Enacted Community

Luke 7

Imagine you're at a dinner party. The host is a respectable church leader and local councilman who lives in a big house on the posh side of town.

Tonight the dinner party is in honor of a visiting speaker. You're glad to have been invited, because there's been a lot of talk about this man. He's been causing something of a stir with his radical views. Some people won't have anything to do with him. But you've got an open mind. It's good to have an opportunity to find out what he's really like.

You hear the doorbell but think nothing of it, until a woman pushes her way into the room. You see the despairing face of the host's wife. This new arrival is wearing a tight-fitting, low-cut blouse; a skirt that's way too short; and stiletto shoes. She's painted up to the nines and totters slightly as she walks—she's probably had one drink too many. She looks like the sort of woman who stands on street corners.

She goes straight to the visiting speaker and throws her arms around him, clasping his head to her bosom. "I'll always be yours," you hear her mumble. She begins to massage his shoulders. It's then that you notice she's crying, her mascara streaking down her cheeks.

Everyone in the room seems to freeze. What a thing for a respectable person to have to endure. You feel for him. How embarrassing.

But instead of pushing her away, he reaches up and puts his arms around her. He says something to her that sounds like, "And you're mine." But he can't have said that. It's obvious what kind of woman she is. He can surely see that for himself. He ought to show some discernment. She might think it's a come-on. Maybe it is. Maybe he's one of her "customers." This visiting speaker clearly has big problems.

Luke tells us about a dinner party much like this.

Luke 7:36–39

One of the Pharisees asked him to eat with him, and he went into the Pharisee's house and took his place at the table. And behold, a woman of the city, who was a sinner, when she learned that he was reclining at table in the Pharisee's house, brought an alabaster flask of ointment, and standing behind him at his feet, weeping, she began to wet his feet with her tears and wiped them with the hair of her head and kissed his feet and anointed them with the ointment. Now when the Pharisee who had invited him saw this, he said to himself, "If this man were a prophet, he would have known who and what sort of woman this is who is touching him, for she is a sinner." (Luke 7:36–39)

Jesus Welcomes Sinners

Luke's presentation of this meal seems to reflect the Greco-Roman *symposium*—a meal followed by an extended discussion. The diners reclined around three sides of a central table on couches, leaving the fourth side open to allow servants access to the table. Bread and wine would be on the table, along with a main dish into which you dipped your bread. Diners lay in a semirecumbent position with their legs out behind them.

Homes in the time of Jesus—especially large homes—had semi-public areas. Some rooms opened onto a courtyard that outsiders could enter. Visitors could see what was happening and even contribute to what was being said. People could readily come in off the streets to pay their respects to the householder or to transact business. The poor, too, might hang around hoping for leftovers.

With this in mind it's easier to picture how this story unfolded. The woman is probably loitering in the public area, and then slips into the dining room and starts rubbing Jesus's feet as they stretch out behind him on the couch.

Except this is no ordinary home. This is the home of a Pharisee, and the Pharisees guarded their purity closely. The Promised Land was defiled by Roman occupation, but at least they could keep their own bodies pure, ready for the day of liberation. So they avoided contact with those they considered impure—like this sinful woman. Although she isn't explicitly called a prostitute, that's what's implied when Luke tells us that she was, literally, "known in the city as a sinner" (v. 37).[1] To the Pharisees she is like an infectious disease. Yet Jesus accepts her. He demonstrates God's grace by welcoming sinners.

And that's okay by us. Christians love a good before-and-after story. You know the sort of thing: "Before I met Christ I was a drug addict and criminal, but now my life has changed."

But this woman treats Jesus with a shocking degree of intimacy. This is not appropriate public behavior. She lets down her hair to wipe her tears from Jesus's feet. In that culture, letting down your hair was what you did in the bedroom. "Letting her hair down in this setting would have been on a par with appearing topless in public."[2] Then the woman kisses Jesus's feet and pours perfume on them. There's even a suggestion that she's treating Jesus as a client, possibly the only way she knows how to relate to men. "Everything about this woman is wrong; she does not belong here and the actions she performs are inappropriate in any setting for someone like Jesus."[3] But Jesus doesn't stop her. He could have said, "I appreciate what you're doing, but it's not really appropriate behavior." He does nothing. As New Testament scholar John Nolland puts it: "Jesus' passivity in the face of this behaviour is extremely eloquent."[4] Prostitution, if that was her business, is a commercial parody of hospitality. But Jesus recognizes her actions as the real thing. He reinterprets what she does as a loving act rather than an erotic act.

Jesus doesn't stop her, even though his reputation is at stake. "When the Pharisee who had invited him saw this, he said to himself, 'If this man were a prophet, he would have known who and what sort of woman this is who is touching him, for she is a sinner'" (Luke 7:39). Jesus is happy to link his identity to hers—just as he is happy to link his identity to yours and mine.

Just before this story Luke recounts the accusation that Jesus is "a friend of sinners." How is Luke going to defend Jesus against this accusation? He doesn't. In fact he tells a story that shows that it's true. Jesus *is* the friend of sinners. He links his identity to ours to reveal himself as the gracious Savior. He comes "eating and drinking" to show that sinners can be part of his kingdom. The glorious Son of Man described in Daniel 7 is the gracious dinner companion of Luke 7.

Luke seems to pick stories involving tax collectors and prostitutes. They exemplify notorious sinners. It's as if he's testing us. Have we grasped God's grace? How do we react when a promiscuous woman kisses the body of Jesus? Do we celebrate God's grace, or are we scandalized? The grace of God turns out to be uncomfortable and embarrassing. Jesus is socially disruptive; his radical grace disrupts social situations. And we don't like church to be disrupted. We regard marginalized people in the church as "a problem" to be "handled."

Involvement with people, especially the marginalized, begins with a profound grasp of God's grace. Often our instincts are to keep our distance. But the Son of God ate with them. He's not embarrassed by them. He lets them kiss his feet. He's the friend of riffraff, traitors, the unrespectable, drunks, druggies, prostitutes, the mentally ill, the broken, and the needy—people whose lives are a mess.

Ultimately Jesus gave his life for them. Luke prefaces the story by telling us that Jesus's enemies accuse him of being "a glutton and drunkard." It's an allusion to Deuteronomy 21:21, which describes how a rebellious, drunken son is to be stoned. Jesus, they are saying, is a rebellious son of Israel. "Yet wisdom is justified by all her children" (Luke 7:35).

In other words, we will see who proves to be the rebellious child. And it turns out not to be Jesus. Jesus will prove to be a faithful Son, indeed *the* faithful Son of Israel. Israel itself is a rebellious son of God.

But here is the crazy irony. Jesus *does* die the death of a rebellious son. Not stoned, but hung on the cross. The same passage in Deuteronomy that condemns a rebellious son declares that everyone who hangs on a tree is cursed (21:22–23). Jesus is not the rebellious son. I am. You are. But Jesus dies the death of a rebellious son. He dies my death. He dies the death of rebellious sinners.

Sinners Welcome Jesus

There are two sides to this story in Luke 7. It's not only a story of Jesus welcoming sinners; it's also a story of a sinner welcoming Jesus. Tim Costello tells how he was looking at this story with a group of drug addicts and prostitutes in Melbourne, Australia. One of the prostitutes said, "Jesus must've been a really great bloke." She could imagine what it was like for this woman. She thought of the formal evenings at the big houses in the posh suburbs of Melbourne. She thought about party-crashing one of those parties, of how she would be treated. She could understand what it cost this woman to anoint the feet of Jesus. She could imagine the repulsion directed toward her by other guests. She could hear the mutterings and see the glares. She could feel the threat of violence. She could understand how much this woman must have loved Jesus.

In 2004 artist Michael Gough created an exhibition entitled "Iconography." An actor dressed as the classic 1950s illustrated ver-

41

sion of Jesus posed around London, blessing passersby on busy streets, with Gough discreetly photographing the results. "No-one engages him in conversation," Gough comments. "People in the City have appointments to honour, meetings to attend, deals to make, lunch to buy." The only person who had time for "Jesus" was the hostess of a strip joint. The only item of her mother's possessions that she'd kept was a little image of Jesus, which she kept by her bed.

Twice Luke tells us that this party took place in the home of a Pharisee (Luke 7:36–37). Luke emphasizes the location. There's no doubt where this is happening. This is Simon's house. And that means Simon is the host. Or is he?

Luke 7:44–50

Then turning toward the woman he said to Simon, "Do you see this woman? I entered your house; you gave me no water for my feet, but she has wet my feet with her tears and wiped them with her hair. You gave me no kiss, but from the time I came in she has not ceased to kiss my feet. You did not anoint my head with oil, but she has anointed my feet with ointment. Therefore I tell you, her sins, which are many, are forgiven—for she loved much. But he who is forgiven little, loves little." And he said to her, "Your sins are forgiven." Then those who were at table with him began to say among themselves, "Who is this, who even forgives sins?" And he said to the woman, "Your faith has saved you; go in peace."

Today a host might shake guests' hands, take their coats, and offer them something to drink. In Jesus's time, you offered water for their feet and greeted them with a kiss. But Simon does none of these things. He is *the host who's not really a host.*

Instead the woman is *the host who's not even a guest.* She's a party-crasher. Jesus contrasts Simon's hospitality with hers:

- *You* gave me no water for my feet, but *she* has wet my feet with her tears and wiped them with her hair.

- *You* gave me no kiss, but from the time I came in *she* has not ceased to kiss my feet.
- *You* did not anoint my head with oil, but *she* has anointed my feet with ointment.

She's the one who welcomed Jesus—not Simon. And it's not even her house. Jesus says: "Do you see this woman?" (v. 44). I think we can safely assume Simon had noticed her! But Jesus is contrasting this woman with "your house." "I am in *your* house, but *she's* been my host."

So why does she do it? Perhaps she sees in Simon's treatment of Jesus something of the way in which she has been treated. Simon is only interested in Jesus for his entertainment value—the eccentric preacher and miracle worker was the must-have guest on the social circuit. He doesn't care for Jesus as a person. This woman could relate to that. She was used to being used by men without respect.

But there's something more going on. Jesus says her faith has saved her (Luke 7:50). What she does is a response of faith to something she's heard or seen in Jesus. Maybe she's met Jesus already. Maybe he's cured her from some sickness. Or maybe she's just heard about his reputation as the friend of sinners. Maybe she's heard him preaching good news to the poor (Luke 7:22–23). Maybe she's heard him telling people not to condemn others, but to forgive (6:37). Maybe she's heard him proclaim blessing to the poor, the hungry, and those who weep (6:20–22). Maybe she's heard that he eats with tax collectors (5:29–32).

What's the difference, then, between these two people? To the onlookers the answer is obvious. One is a righteous, respectable man; the other is a degraded, sinful woman who sells herself for money. But Jesus sees things altogether differently. When Simon condemns Jesus, Jesus responds not by defending his actions, but by explaining hers.

Luke 7:40–43

And Jesus answering said to him, "Simon, I have something to say to you."
And he answered, "Say it, Teacher."
"A certain moneylender had two debtors. One owed five hundred denarii,
and the other fifty. When they could not pay, he cancelled the debt of both.
Now which of them will love him more?" Simon answered, "The one, I
suppose, for whom he cancelled the larger debt." And he said to him, "You
have judged rightly."

The principle is simple. If someone forgives you, you'll love them. If someone forgives you a lot, you'll love them a lot. Even Simon concedes this. And this woman clearly loves Jesus a lot. Her audacity, her tears, and her affection for Jesus make that clear. So Jesus can say with confidence that her sins are forgiven.

But what about Simon? Simon hasn't even shown the normal courtesies of a host to Jesus, and he's despised this poor woman. He hasn't shown love. The only conclusion can be that he's been forgiven little—and probably not at all. Simon is not only a legalist, but has structured his world around his legalism. Meals express inclusion. But this meal has been warped by legalism. Simon wants his meals to express the wrong kind of inclusion. Simon thinks he's invited the righteous, so the unrighteous are forced to party-crash. But Jesus reveals that Simon's definition of righteousness is upside down.

Simon decides Jesus can't be a prophet, because Jesus doesn't seem to have the God-given insight to see the true character of this woman. But Simon is in for a shock. Jesus can see what kind of woman she is—he acknowledges that her sins are many—but she's forgiven. More than that, Jesus can see into Simon's heart to know what he's thinking. Luke writes, "He said to himself. . . . And Jesus answering said to him. . . ." Jesus replies to Simon's thoughts as if he had spoken them aloud. But the real shock is this: Jesus sees the heart of this woman and he sees the heart of Simon—and he's more disgusted by what he sees in Simon's heart than by what he sees in the woman's heart.

Simon's attitude to this woman exposes his heart. It's always like that. Problem people, difficult people, different people have a habit of exposing our hearts. Behavior always comes from the desires of the heart—Jesus says as much in the previous chapter (Luke 6:43–45). When a fellow ministry leader and I faced a difficult situation, he said, "What I find most disappointing is what it has revealed about my own heart. It's shown me again that I still need people's approval, because I fear them more than I fear God." When someone is difficult, disappointing, or disrespectful, your reaction reveals your own heart. If you react with anger or bitterness, then your "need" for control or respect or success is exposed. If you're trusting God's sovereignty rather than your own abilities, and if you're concerned for God's glory rather than your own reputation, then it will be a different story. When you discover that someone in your church has fallen into sin, your own heart will be exposed. You may discover grace in your heart from God. But you may also discover pride and self-righteousness.

Whenever we look down on someone for being smelly, or disorganized, or lazy, or emotional, or promiscuous, or socially inept, or bitter, then we're like graceless Simon. And if we look down on people for not understanding grace, then we are like graceless Simon. If you're thinking about how this applies to someone else, then you're like Simon. Jesus says to us, "If you look down on others, you love little, because you understand so little of your sin and my grace."

The difference between Simon and the woman is not just how they view Jesus. It's also how they view themselves. Simon has no sense of forgiveness, because he has no sense of need. But the woman has a strong sense of her brokenness. She knows her life is a mess. And she sees Jesus as someone who accepts her anyway. So she has an overwhelming love for him—a love that risks social disgrace.

Involvement with people, especially the marginalized, must begin with a sense of God's grace. But not just God's grace to them, but his grace to *me*. I need to be melted and broken by grace. When I speak

45

with someone who's an alcoholic or a single mother, or someone who's depressed or unemployed or unemployable, I must do so as a fellow sinner. We're all broken people in a broken world. If I do not understand this, then my good intentions will be patronizing. Anything I say will be heard as "become like me." Only as I'm daily struck by God's amazing grace to me, Tim Chester, will my life and words point to Jesus as the Savior.

*

In his book, *Bowling Alone*, Robert Putman reveals that there's been a 33 percent decrease in families eating together over the last three decades.[5] And more than half of those families are watching television as they eat together. Over the same period there's been a 45 percent decline in entertaining friends. Growing up I would ask each Sunday, "Who's coming for dinner today?" Not *whether* but *who*, because I knew my parents always would have invited someone. "In the typical American household, the average number of dinners eaten together is three per week, with the average length of dinner being 20 minutes."[6] Many homes no longer even have a dining room. We protect ourselves from outsiders, but our security systems and garden gates are our prisons, cutting us off from community. Instead we get our community vicariously through soap operas. *Friends* is a television program or a Facebook number, not people with whom we eat and laugh and cry.

Instead we've commercialized hospitality. In his history of Starbucks, Taylor Clark argues that the secret of Starbucks's success is not in its coffee, but "the pull of the coffeehouse as a *place*."[7] When sociologist Roy Oldenburg coined the term "third place" to describe a neutral gathering spot that's neither home or work, "the company," Clark writes, "now had its philanthropic rallying cry: it wasn't a coffee company, but a third place bringing people together through the social glue of coffee."[8] Starbucks's research showed that people wanted "a cozy social atmosphere above all else. . . . For those seeking a refuge from the world, the cup of coffee they bought was really just the price of admission to partake of the coffeehouse scene."[9] Starbucks is selling us hospitality.

Hotels were the first to commercialize hospitality. In the past ordinary households opened their homes to strangers. In the Medieval period monasteries provided a resting place for travelers and cared for the ill. We get the word "hospital" from their "hospitality" to the sick. "In pre-industrial cities, public eateries were classless, and rich and poor often shared the same table, just as they lived together in the same street."[10] But a new breed of eating-house, the restaurant, originating in Paris, broke from this. "Restaurants presented an entirely new way of eating out. Anyone, including women, could go there at any time of day, sit at their own table, order what they liked off a menu, and pay for it separately."[11] Public dining could now be done in isolation. Now television shows and cookbooks sell the idea of hospitality back to us as they encourage us to remake hospitality in the image of restaurant cuisine. Sharing a family meal has been replaced by the fancy dinner party.

There's nothing wrong with eating out or hosting a special meal—indeed there's a lot right with it. But somewhere along the line the commercialization of meals has cost us something precious. Hospitality has become performance art, and we've lost the creation of intimacy around a meal.

Meals as Enacted Community

Hospitality involves welcoming, creating space, listening, paying attention, and providing. Meals slow things down. Some of us don't like that. We like to get things done. But meals force you to be people oriented instead of task oriented. Sharing a meal is not the only way to build relationships, but it is number one on the list.

It's possible to remain at a distance from someone in public gatherings—even in a Bible study. Meals bring you close. You see people *in situ*, in life, as they are. You connect and communicate. Novelist

Barbara Kingsolver describes dinnertime as "the cornerstone of our family's mental health." "If I had to quantify it," she says, "I'd say 75 percent of my crucial parenting effort has taken place during or surrounding the time our family convenes for our evening meal."[12] Generous hospitality leads to reconciliation. It expresses forgiveness. Unresolved conflict can't be ignored when we gather round the meal table; you can't eat in silence without realizing there's an issue to address. Paul uses hospitality as a metaphor for reconciliation when he says to the Corinthians: "Make room in your hearts for us. We have wronged no one . . ." (2 Cor. 7:2). Hospitality can be a kind of sacrament of forgiveness.

Marzipan cake. That's how my friend Chris knew his mother-in-law had finally accepted him into the family. Now every cake she bakes for him is a reaffirmation of that acceptance. It makes the cake doubly sweet. That's how food so often works. We enjoy food not just because of the taste, but because of the companionship and welcome it expresses. Indeed sometimes we enjoy food despite the taste because of the love in which it's packaged. "Better is a dinner of herbs where love is than a fattened ox and hatred with it" (Prov. 15:17).

Many people love the idea of the church as a community. But when we eat together, we encounter not some theoretical community, but real people with all their problems and quirks. The meal table is an opportunity to give up our proud ideals by which we judge others and accept in their place the real community created by the cross of Christ, with all its brokenness. It's easy to love people in some abstract sense and preach the virtues of love. But we're called to love the real individuals sitting around the table.

"Those who dream of this idealized community," Dietrich Bonhoeffer warns, "demand that it be fulfilled by God, by others, and by themselves. They enter the community of Christians with their demands, set up their own law, and judge one another and even God accordingly." But, Bonhoeffer says, "Christian community is not an ideal we have to realize, but rather a reality created by God in Christ in which we may participate." So "we enter into that life together with other Christians, not as those who make demands, but as those who thankfully receive. . . . We do not complain about what God does not give us; rather we are thankful for what God does give us daily." This means that the disillusionment we experience when we encounter real people with their problems is a reminder that we "can never live by our own words and deeds, but only by that one Word and deed that really binds us together, the forgiveness of sins in Jesus Christ."[13]

Hospitality will lead to "collateral damage." Food will be spilled on your carpet. You'll be left with clearing up. Your pantry may be decimated. But remember that God is welcoming you into his home through the blood of his own Son. The hospitality of God embodied in the table fellowship of Jesus is a celebration and sign of his grace and generosity. And we're to imitate that generosity.

Meals also have the power to shape and reshape community. A person to whom we may have related in one role becomes a person to whom we relate as friend. Serving another changes the dynamics of a relationship. The leader who serves at table is no longer aloof.

Meals indicate social status, and they thereby allow us to transform social status. They're a microcosm of social reality that we can manipulate. "Food is a social substance and currency. What one is able (and chooses) to serve expresses one's own position and helps define one's relationship to others. What you, the guest, are offered is a measure of your standing in the eyes of society and your host."[14] This is what Jesus is doing in eating with the marginalized. The marginalized cease to be marginal when they're included around a meal table. The lonely cease to be lonely. The alien ceases to be alien. Strangers become friends.

We live in a graceless culture. Not a graceless world: every bird-song, every kindness, and every meal is a sign of God's ongoing grace toward his creation. But we live in a graceless culture of competition in which we're all trying to get ahead. It's a culture of insecurity in which we're all trying to prove ourselves. We hold grudges, envy success, protect ourselves. In the race to the top you either tread on the competition or they will tread on you. In contrast to the God of Exodus 34:6–7, we're unforgiving and quick to anger. We measure out our love, hold grudges, and get away with whatever we can. Look into the faces of the people on the subway and see the toll the rat race takes on its victims.

In this culture our shared meals offer a moment of grace. A sign of something different. A pointer to God's coming world. "Life in the kingdom . . . demands that we adopt a new set of table manners, and as we observe this etiquette, we become increasingly civilized according to the codes of the city of God."[15] Around the table we offer friendship and celebrate life. Our meals offer a divine moment, an opportunity for people to be seduced by grace into a better life, a truer life, and a more human existence.

Church as a Meal

Meals were central to the life of the apostolic churches: "Day by day, attending the temple together and breaking bread in their homes, they received their food with glad and generous hearts" (Acts 2:46). The only local church gathering the book of Acts describes concerns the church at Troas. We read that they "were gathered together to break bread" (Acts 20:7; see also v. 11). They met for a meal.

In 1 Corinthians 11 Paul has to correct the excesses of Corinthian church gatherings, because the rich aren't waiting for the poor or providing for them. The Corinthian believers met around a meal, but in a dysfunctional manner that didn't reflect the gospel. Paul's answer, however, is not to abolish the meal, but to realign it to the cross.

The first churches met in homes. Most houses could accommodate thirty to forty people at gatherings, although in larger houses it's conceivable that groups of a hundred could have gathered to eat.[16] There's evidence that by the mid-second century, houses were being adapted as church buildings. Specially built church buildings only really take off when the Roman Empire officially becomes Christian, and churches begin to be built in the style of Roman temples. But during the apostolic period churches met in homes, around a meal.

The New Testament commonly portrays churches as families, with God as Father, Jesus as older brother, and other members as brothers and sisters. Church leaders are family leaders, and must prove their ability to manage their own households before they can manage the household of God. One of the requirements for elders is that they must be "hospitable" (1 Tim. 3:2; Titus 1:8; see Rom. 16:23). Consider that many requirements churches typically have for leaders (like a seminary degree) are not required by Paul in 1 Timothy 3 and Titus 1. But what he does require is that they be hospitable. Perhaps this was because church meetings were family meals. How could you lead a meal-meeting if you weren't hospitable? How could you extend the generous welcome of the gospel if you didn't welcome people into your home?

The meetings of the apostolic churches were shared meals. It's not that they sometimes had a church lunch, or that they had some food before or after their meetings. Their meetings were meals. The second-century theologian Tertullian describes a church gathering:

Our feast explains itself by its name. The Greeks call it *agape*, i.e. affection. Whatever it costs, our outlay in the name of piety is gain, since with the good things of the feast we benefit the needy. . . . The participants, before reclining, taste first of prayer to God. As much is eaten as satisfies the cravings of hunger; as much is drunk as befits the chaste. . . . After manual ablution, and the bringing in of lights, each is asked to stand forth and sing, as he can, a hymn to God, either one from the holy Scriptures or one of his own composing. . . . As the feast commenced with prayer, so with prayer it is closed.[17]

Christians also provided hospitality to fellow believers who were travelling. This was how they received news from other churches and expressed unity with them. Itinerant teachers travelled from church to church to build them up, and teachers were to be offered hospitality (3 John 5–8). But John warns his readers not to show hospitality to false teachers: "If anyone comes to you and does not bring this teaching, do not receive him into your house or give him any greeting, for whoever greets him takes part in his wicked works" (2 John 10–11). Does not receiving him into your house mean refusing him a bed for the night or refusing to let him address your house church? Probably both, since church is so closely aligned with house, and hospitality so closely aligned with fellowship.

The withdrawal of hospitality is the ultimate sanction of the church community: "But now I am writing to you not to associate with anyone who bears the name of brother if he is guilty of sexual immorality or greed, or is an idolater, reviler, drunkard, or swindler—not even to eat with such a one" (1 Cor. 5:11). Paul is calling on the church in Corinth to discipline a member of the church who, it seems, was sleeping with his father's wife. We would describe this discipline as "excommunication." Paul talks about delivering him over to Satan and not associating with him (5:5). But the concrete form this takes—the only one mentioned—is not eating with him. Paul is quick to clarify that we can eat with unbelieving sinners; such eating is a missional act. The discipline is for someone who claims to be a believer, but acts like an unbeliever without any sign of repentance. The sanction only makes sense if meals are integral to church life, and church itself is to some extent embodied through shared meals. You might like to consider how quickly an unrepentant church member would notice the church's discipline if he or she stopped receiving hospitality in your church.

One New Testament letter was written specifically to address the issue of with whom you can eat. In Galatians, Paul says: "When Cephas came to Antioch, I opposed him to his face, because he stood condemned. For before certain men came from James, he was eating with the Gentiles; but when they came he drew back and separated himself, fearing the circumcision party. . . . But when I saw that their conduct was not in step with the truth of the gospel, I said to Cephas before them all, 'If you, though a Jew, live like a Gentile and not like a Jew, how can you force the Gentiles to live like Jews?'" (Gal. 2:11–14).

Our meals express our doctrine of justification. It's possible to articulate an orthodox theology of justification by faith, but communicate through your meals a doctrine of justification by works. This may well be what was happening in Galatia. Paul's opponents in Galatia were probably saying something like this to Gentiles: "It's great that you've been saved by faith in Jesus. But if you really want to belong to God's people, then you need to be circumcised. Until then, we can't eat with you." Paul attacks this false logic. If we make law the basis on which we eat with one another, then we're operating with a doctrine of justification by works (Gal. 2:11–21). If you start down this route, then you need to keep the whole law (5:2–4), and we know none of us can do that (2:15–16). But "in Christ Jesus you are all sons of God, through faith" (3:26).

In classic buddy movies two people are thrown together, typically as police partners. At first their stark differences create conflict. But after going through a life-and-death experience together, they become deep, lifelong friends. The church is a community full of differences that humanly speaking ought to result in conflict. But we have a shared life-and-death experience. We're sharers in the death and resurrection of Jesus. His death is our death and his life is our life. Nothing expresses this more than baptism (Rom. 6:2–3). Now this life-and-death experience binds us together in community: "For as many of you as were baptized into Christ have put on Christ. There is neither Jew nor Greek, there is neither slave nor free, there is no male or female, for you are all one in Christ Jesus"

(Gal. 3:27–28). And that means there can be no distinctions around the meal table.

A Table under a Tree

In the closing scene of the Civil War film *Cold Mountain*, which is based on the novel by Charles Frazier, a meal is spread under a tree. Around the table are the assorted characters that have populated the story. There's Ruby, a tough woman from a tough background whose mother died when she was a child and whose father neglected her. She's there with her husband, Georgia, an ex-soldier, and their two children. But present, too, is her father, who is also back from the war and to whom she's at last been reconciled. There's Sally, who can't speak because she watched profiteering home guardsmen torture and murder her family.

And there's Ada, the central character. At the beginning of the film she has a brief romance with a young man called Inman, with whom she shares a single kiss before he goes away to join the Confederate army. At first she is refined and aloof, but when her father, the local minister, dies, she has to adapt to country life through a growing partnership with Ruby, her social opposite. Meanwhile the film follows Inman's danger-strewn journey home to Ada. They're reunited for one day, when they unofficially marry, before Inman, too, is murdered.

Broken people have found family and some measure of healing together. This is what we see around the meal table under the tree at the end of *Cold Mountain*. And this image is repeated again and again in Luke's Gospel. Here's the community of the broken gathered around a meal, finding hope in the grace of Jesus. This is what church is to be: a community of broken people finding family around a meal under the tree of Calvary.

There is one final character around the table in *Cold Mountain*. Ada's one night of marriage with Inman has given her a child. Her name is Grace.

3

Meals as Enacted Hope

Luke 9

Luke 9:7–20

Now Herod the tetrarch heard about all that was happening, and he was per-
plexed, because it was said by some that John had been raised from the dead,
by some that Elijah had appeared, and by others that one of the prophets of old
had risen. Herod said, "John I beheaded, but who is this about whom I hear
such things?" And he sought to see him.

On their return the apostles told [Jesus] all that they had done. And he took
them and withdrew apart to a town called Bethsaida. When the crowds learned
it, they followed him, and he welcomed them and spoke to them of the kingdom
of God and cured those who had need of healing. Now the day began to wear
away, and the twelve came and said to him, "Send the crowd away to go into the
surrounding villages and countryside to find lodging and get provisions, for we are
here in a desolate place." But he said to them, "You give them something to eat."
They said, "We have no more than five loaves and two fish—unless we are to go
and buy food for all these people." For there were about five thousand men. And he
said to his disciples, "Have them sit down in groups of about fifty each." And they
did so, and had them all sit down. And taking the five loaves and the two fish, he
looked up to heaven and said a blessing over them. Then he broke the loaves and
gave them to the disciples to set before the crowd. And they all ate and were satisfied.
And what was left over was picked up, twelve baskets of broken pieces.

Now it happened that as he was praying alone, the disciples were with him.
And he asked them, "Who do the crowds say that I am?" And they answered,

"John the Baptist. But others say, Elijah, and others, that one of the prophets of old has risen." Then he said to them, "But who do you say that I am?" And Peter answered, "The Christ of God."

"Who is this about whom I hear such things?" That's the question King Herod asks. The answer given by the people who shared their lives with Jesus was this: "the Christ of God" (Luke 9:20). "Christ" isn't a name. Jesus wasn't "Mr. Christ." "Christ" is the Greek translation of the Hebrew word "Messiah." It means "Anointed One." Jewish kings were anointed with oil, so "the Christ" was how Jews referred to God's promised Savior-King—the one they hoped would rescue God's people and put the world right. But how can we know that Jesus is the Messiah?

In verses 7–9 Luke gives us three possible answers to the question of Jesus's identity. Jesus could be John the Baptist raised from the dead. Second, he could be Elijah. That might seem a bit random to us, but the Bible says Elijah was taken up to heaven in a chariot (2 Kings 2:1–12). Elijah didn't die in the ordinary sense, and the Jews wondered whether he might come back to prepare the way for the Messiah (Mal. 4:5–6; Mark 9:11–13). Third, maybe Jesus is "one of the prophets of old." Moses had promised that one day a prophet like Moses would come (Deut. 18:17–19). So maybe Jesus is a new Moses.

We get exactly the same three options when Jesus asks the question of his disciples in verses 18–20: a new John, a new Elijah, or a new Moses. And right in the middle Luke placed the story of the feeding of the five thousand. Why? Because this feeding provides the crucial clue to the identity of Jesus. What makes the difference between Herod's unanswered question and Jesus's answered question is this party in the wilderness.

Mark links Peter's spiritual recognition of Jesus to the miraculous cure of a blind man (Mark 8:17–30). In Matthew Jesus says his Father has revealed to Peter that Jesus is the Christ (Matt. 16:16–17). In

Luke Jesus is revealed around a meal—just as he will be in Emmaus on the first Easter day (Luke 24:30–32). Here in our passage, Jesus offers hospitality: "He welcomed them" (Luke 9:11). Although our English translations say "sit" in verse 15, the word could be translated "reclined"; Luke says the crowd reclined on the grass just as they would at a meal. This is more than a picnic; this is a banquet with Jesus as the host. Jesus is known through his catering.

A New Moses

Three important echoes of the Old Testament in this story point to the identity of Jesus. The first is God's provision of manna. Hundreds of years before, God had rescued his people from slavery in Egypt. But soon the people were complaining about a lack of food. So God sent manna: "I am about to rain bread from heaven for you" (Ex. 16:4). The people in Luke 9 are again in a wilderness without food (Luke 9:12). And Jesus looks up to heaven, and bread miraculously comes down (v. 16).

So Jesus is a new Moses about to lead a new exodus, to rescue God's people from sin and death. When Jesus is transfigured eight days after the feeding of the five thousand, with Moses and Elijah, they talk about "his departure" or literally "his exodus" (Luke 9:31). But there's more.

A New Elijah

The feeding of the five thousand would have reminded people of a second Old Testament story.

Elisha told his servant to feed a group of prophets with twenty loaves. "But his servant said, 'How can I set this before a hundred men?' So he repeated, 'Give them to the men, that they may eat, for thus says the LORD, "They shall eat and have some left."' So he set it before them. And they ate and had some left, according to the word of the LORD" (2 Kings 4:42–44).

Elisha tells his servant, "You feed them." The man protests. But there's not only enough, there's leftovers. And now Jesus tells the disciples. "You feed them." They protest. But there's not only enough, there are twelve baskets full of leftovers.

When Elijah was taken up to heaven, Elisha took his cloak as a sign that he was Elijah's successor. He was the new Elijah. So for Jesus to be doing things like Elisha was to suggest he might be the new Elijah.

So maybe Jesus is the new Elijah who provides for God's people. Maybe. But he's more than that. Peter says Jesus is "the Christ of God." That's because the feeding has a third Old Testament resonance.

A Messianic Banquet
Eight hundred years before Jesus, the prophet Isaiah proclaimed this promise from God:

> On this mountain the LORD of hosts will make for all peoples
>   a feast of rich food, a feast of well-aged wine,
>   of rich food full of marrow, of aged wine well refined.
> And he will swallow up on this mountain
>   the covering that is cast over all peoples,
>   the veil that is spread over all nations.
> He will swallow up death forever;
> and the Lord GOD will wipe away tears from all faces,
>   and the reproach of his people he will take away from all the
>   earth,
>   for the LORD has spoken.
> It will be said on that day,
>   "Behold, this is our God; we have waited for him, that he
>   might save us.
>   This is the LORD; we have waited for him;
>   let us be glad and rejoice in his salvation." (Isa. 25:6–9)

When my friend Peter turned eighty, his son took him out for a birthday meal. His son is a top surgeon, so they went to a top restaurant. Peter told me that none of the menus had prices except his son's. It was a sumptuous, delicious, perfect banquet—and an expensive one. But God will provide a lavish feast to surpass any five-star restaurant. What's more, God's menu also has no prices on it, because the price has already been paid through the precious blood of Jesus. Now we are invited to feast without money:

> Come, everyone who thirsts,
>> come to the waters;
> and he who has no money,
>> come, buy and eat!
> Come, buy wine and milk
>> without money and without price.
> Why do you spend your money for that which is not bread,
>> and your labor for that which does not satisfy?
> Listen diligently to me, and eat what is good,
>> and delight yourselves in rich food. (Isa. 55:1–2)

That's not all. No one need ever leave this feast. In Isaiah 25 death itself is on the menu—God himself will swallow it up. So this is a perpetual feast. In Luke 9 the disciples want to send the people away. But Jesus makes it possible for them to stay. No one need leave this feast. There's more food at the end than at the beginning. This has the makings of a perpetual feast.

This feast is known as "the messianic banquet." God's Messiah will defeat death, put the world right, and enable us to enjoy God's presence. It's a wonderful description of God's coming world—of its provision and plenty and satisfaction.

The feeding of five thousand people was not the full deal. But it was a glimpse of it. Jesus is the host of God's great party, just as he was the host of the dinner in this wilderness. When Jesus saw the crowd "he welcomed them" (Luke 9:11). Jesus is God's Messiah, because he welcomes us to the messianic banquet. This is what confirms Jesus's identity.

That's all well and good for the disciples. They were there. They ate the bread. They collected the leftovers. But is it credible for us? After all, that sort of thing doesn't happen in our world.

But that's the point. Our world is a world of hunger, pain, suffering, and want. Even in neighborhoods where most people have enough to eat, we still live in want. We're still unsatisfied. We may not long for bread, but we long for meaning, intimacy, fulfillment, community, purpose, and joy. We long for the world to be sorted out.

Jesus doesn't fit in our world. He breaks down our categories. He bursts our expectations. His actions do not fit the laws and expectations of this world. To judge them by the standards of this world is a category mistake. To judge them by your experience is to miss the point. They don't belong in this world because they give us a glimpse of *another* world. Jesus's coming was the start of a new world. His actions were a sign of God's coming world.

The world we rule over is a world where famine can strike, injustice goes unchecked, war ravages nations, communities fracture, and families divide. Welcome to the kingdom of me. And you.

Welcome to the kingdom of Herod. Mark puts the story of the feeding of the five thousand immediately after the story of another party (Mark 6). Herod holds a birthday banquet for himself to impress his nobles. The climax is an erotic dance by his stepdaughter. Then Herod is manipulated into having John the Baptist murdered. Jesus welcomes everyone to his party. The poor are included. Jesus's motivation is compassion. He proclaims good news. And the party ends with everyone satisfied. Herod, in contrast, only welcomes the in-crowd. The poor are excluded. He is motivated by pride and enslaved by his need to save face. Herod's party ends in death.

In Luke's Gospel, Mary sees in God's choice of her, despite her "humble estate" (Luke 1:48), a sign of what's coming: "He has brought down the mighty from their thrones and exalted those of humble estate; he has filled the hungry with good things, and the rich he has sent away empty" (1:52–53). Now in this desolate place the humble and hungry are satisfied (Luke 9:17), while the mighty on their thrones seek Jesus, but cannot see him (9:9).

Jesus himself proclaims: "Blessed are you who are poor, for yours is the kingdom of God. Blessed are you who are hungry now, for you shall be satisfied . . ." (Luke 6:20–21). The tenses are important. Are hungry now. Shall be satisfied. This is the promise of a coming kingdom and a coming feast. The poor, the broken, and the hungry who recognize their need and turn to Jesus will one day receive the kingdom and enjoy his eternal banquet.

But here in this desolate place in Luke 9, for a moment in history, we are given a glimpse of that coming reality. Five thousand hungry men "all ate and were satisfied" (Luke 9:17). This is not the real thing. Five thousand is a lot of people, but it's not all God's people. And these people would soon be hungry again. But while it wasn't the real thing, it was a foretaste of the real thing. The twelve baskets of leftovers are a sign that this feast will continue.

In this desolate place as a group of needy people gather together and share food, with Jesus at the center and with Jesus as the provider, we see God's coming world glimpsed right here, right now.

When your church family gathers together as a group of needy people and shares food with Jesus at the center and with Jesus as the provider, you glimpse God's coming world right here, right now.

The Christian community is the beginning and sign of God's coming world—and no more so than when we eat together. Our meals are a foretaste of the future messianic banquet. Our meals reveal the identity of Jesus. Our meals are a proclamation and demonstration of God's good news.

Jesus Provides for Us in Mission

I don't know if you've ever been asked to cater for a large group of people. It's a big headache. You have to ensure that you have enough food, that special dietary requirements are considered, and that the food's properly cooked and ready at the right time. Imagine being asked to do all that when you have no food! Jesus asks the disciples to do an impossible task. They feel totally underresourced. But Jesus completes the task.

I think Luke tells the story of feeding the five thousand to bring out the responsibility of the disciples and their inability. Just before this story, Jesus sends them out on mission and tells them not to take any bread (Luke 9:3). Now they must rustle up bread from nowhere—and not just for themselves, but for a crowd of people. In the other Gospels the reference to five thousand men comes at the end of the story to emphasize Jesus's *ability* to provide. Luke mentions this detail earlier in the story, where the disciples are asked to feed the crowd, to emphasize their *inability*. Then there are the twelve baskets of leftovers—one for each for the disciples—to remind them that Jesus provides.

Jesus is preparing the disciples for his absence (Luke 9:37–43). The day is coming when he will give them—as he gives us—another impossible task: to proclaim repentance and forgiveness to all nations (24:45–49). What can we do? Jesus asks us what resources we have, and he asks us to have faith. That day the disciples took home twelve baskets full of leftover food. The impossible task was not only completed, but was overcompleted! And those twelve disciples are now two billion disciples and counting.

We need a theology of leftovers. The Old Testament people of Israel were told to gather just enough manna for one day (Exodus 16). When they tried to gather two days' worth, it always went bad. If you acted as if manna was a finite resource that must be hoarded, then it went bad. You could only consume it by trusting it to be an infinite resource from God. The disciples thought their five loaves were a finite resource that couldn't be shared. Five thousand people later, they still had twelve baskets full of bread.

Can you reach your neighborhood with the gospel? Can you pluck up the courage to tell your friends about Jesus? Can you start a new church in your city? Can you feed five thousand people with five loaves?

"We could never do that; we don't have the money or people." Jesus says, "What do you have? Offer that to me, and let me use it for my glory." The early church father Cyril of Alexandria said:

> There were also gathered twelve baskets of fragments. And what do we infer from this? A plain assurance that hospitality receives a rich recompense from God. . . . Let nothing, therefore, prevent willing people from receiving strangers. . . . Let no one say, "I do not possess suitable means. What I can do is altogether trifling and insufficient for many." Receive strangers, my beloved. Overcome that reluctance which wins no reward. The Savior will multiply the little you have many times beyond expectation. Although you give but little, you will receive much. For he that sows blessings shall also reap blessings, according to the blessed Paul's words [2 Corinthians 9:6].[1]

When it comes right down to it, the disciples can't provide for the people. They have the power of Jesus, but it's his power. They share the ministry of Jesus, but it's his ministry. It's easy for us to play at being messiah. We want to help, and it's right that we do show love, as the context demands (Luke 10:25–37). But we need to be careful not to think we can solve people's problems for them. It's not good for us; if we try to save the world, we'll quickly burn out. And it's not good for the people we help; people need to be helped to cope for themselves rather than become reliant on us. Reliance on us might feed our egos, but it doesn't bring lasting change. But even more importantly, Christ is the Savior—not us. Our role is to point to him. We have a responsibility to welcome people to the messianic banquet. But we can't bring them in. What we offer people is Jesus. His death is sufficient and complete. He is the Provider. He is the host. Not us.

When Jesus sends out the twelve, he tells them not to take a staff, bag, or bread, and he tells them to stay wherever they're welcomed

(Luke 9:3). But the days when God's messengers can expect a welcome are numbered. John the Baptist's death is a pointer of what's coming (v. 9). On the night before his own death Jesus reminds the disciples of the time when he sent them out without money. He says: "But now let the one who has a moneybag take it, and likewise a knapsack. And let the one who has no sword sell his cloak and buy one. For I tell you that this Scripture must be fulfilled in me: 'And he was numbered with the transgressors.' For what is written about me has its fulfillment" (22:35–37). In other words, the days when you could expect to be welcomed are no more. The Messiah is about to be treated like a transgressor, and this is how his followers can expect to be treated. From now on you can't rely on general goodwill. You must be prepared. But, while the world may not welcome us, Jesus provides for us.

Jesus Provides for Us through the Cross

"Taking the five loaves and the two fish and looking up to heaven, he gave thanks and broke them. Then he gave them to the disciples to set before the people" (Luke 9:16, NIV). When Luke describes the Last Supper, he writes: "And [Jesus] took bread, gave thanks and broke it, and gave it to them, saying, 'This is my body given for you; do this in remembrance of me'" (22:19, NIV).

Taking, thanking, breaking, giving—the same words in the same order. Luke is making a connection. Jesus is the Messiah who provides for God's people and hosts God's great banquet. Ultimately he provides by dying and he welcomes us because he was abandoned. As soon as he is acclaimed as the Messiah, he explains that he must suffer and die (Luke 9:20–22, 43–45). Jesus is the Messiah, but he's not the Messiah people expect. He won't conquer the Roman army and liberate Jerusalem. There will be judgment, but it will fall on him. He'll be judged in our place, so that we can escape God's judgment and be welcomed to God's great feast.

Eight days after Jesus warns of his coming suffering and death, he is transfigured, and a voice speaks from heaven (Luke 9:28–36). What does the Father say? It's a bit of surprise. As Jesus is transfigured in glory, we might expect the Father to say, "This is my Son, gaze upon him." But the Father says, "Listen to him." And what has Jesus just been saying? That he is the Messiah who will be crucified.

In Luke 9:51 the Gospel heads off in a new direction—literally. "When the days drew near for him to be taken up, he set his face to go to Jerusalem." All the action in chapters 1–9 takes place in Galilee. But now we're heading to Jerusalem and the cross. So the feeding of the five thousand comes at the end of the first half of the Gospel. This open-air, large-scale meal is the climax of part 1: Jesus is the Christ. The rest of the Gospel spells out what it means for Jesus to be the Christ and what it means to follow this Christ. He is the Christ who must die (Luke 9:21–22, 43–45), and to follow him means a life of death to self and service of others (vv. 23–27, 46–48).

Jesus is the host of God's banquet, and he provides for us by dying for us. This means we shouldn't look for repeat performances. Jesus can do miraculous things today. I've heard amazing stories of God's provision—of food appearing where there was no food. But we shouldn't expect these things as the norm. These are not the fulfillment of God's promise of a messianic banquet. We should look to the cross. That's where God provides for us: "Jesus then said to them, 'Truly, truly, I say to you, it was not Moses who gave you the bread from heaven, but my Father gives you the true bread from heaven. . . . I am the living bread that came down from heaven. If anyone eats of this bread, he will live forever. And the bread that I will give for the life of the world is my flesh'" (John 6:32, 51).

Taking the Loaves, He Gave Thanks

October 2010. Fresh New England lobster and clams. Alaskan salmon caught by a friend. Wild moose shot by our host. All of it cooked outside and eaten in a cabin by the waterside. This was not a typical meal in my home. This was my treat after speaking at a conference in Maine. Delicious food. A beautiful location. Great company. A wonderful expression of God's goodness.

"Taking the five loaves and the two fish and looking up to heaven, [Jesus] gave thanks and broke them. Then he gave them to the disciples to set before the people" (9:16, NIV). The feeding of the five thousand not only looks forward in hope to the messianic banquet. In receiving the bread with thanksgiving, Jesus affirms the goodness of creation. And by affirming the goodness of God's creation as he promises a new world, Jesus reminds us that this world is not going to be trashed, but redeemed. Food matters because it is part of God's good creation and part of God's new creation.

Consider for a moment what happens at the feeding of the five thousand. God gives out bread. On a massive scale. Or think about the wedding at Cana. Jesus turns perhaps 120–180 gallons of water into wine. Quality wine. At the beginning of the Bible story, the first thing God does for humanity is present us with a menu: "The LORD God planted a garden in Eden, in the east, and there he put the man whom he had formed. And out of the ground the LORD God made to spring up every tree that is pleasant to the sight and good for food" (Gen. 2:8–9). At the end of the Bible story, God sets before us a perpetual feast. God likes doing the catering. He thinks food is a good thing.

God incarnate eats. Jesus would have eaten two meals a day. When he ate with the rich, he might have had white bread, but most of the time he ate the barley bread eaten by the poor, along with cheese, butter, and eggs. Meat and poultry were too expensive to be eaten except on feast days. He may have had fish on the Sabbath. There was of course no tea or coffee. Jesus would have drunk wine, generally mixed with three-parts water. Honey was the primary sweetener, along with figs. Pepper, ginger, and other spices were imported, but were expensive.[2] Such was the diet of God incarnate.

The risen Christ eats. Indeed he makes a point of doing so publicly: "They gave him a piece of broiled fish, and he took it and ate before them" (Luke 24:42–43). Eating in the presence of God is our future. Food will be part of the renewed creation. Food is not left behind with the resurrection. References to a future feast are not just metaphors for an ethereal future existence. Our future is a real feast.

The point is that food isn't just fuel. It's not just a mechanism for sustaining us for ministry. It's gift, generosity, grace. Jesus gave thanks and broke bread. In so doing, he affirms that food is to be received as a gift from God. Food matters as matter. It's a physical substance, and part of God's good world. We're to embrace the world as it is— not merely as a picture of some other spiritual world.

Food is a central ingredient in our experience of God's goodness. It's not merely an illustration of God's goodness. If it were a mere illustration, we could leave it behind once we'd gotten the idea. Food is goodness.

Since [God] does not need [creation], its whole reason for being must lie in its own goodness; He has no use for it; only delight. Just think what that means. We were not made in God's image for nothing. The child's preference for sweets over spinach, mankind's universal love of the toothsome rather than the nutritious is the mark of our greatness. . . . We have eyes which see what He sees, lips which praise what He praises, and mouths which relish things, because He first pronounced them [good]. The world is no disposable ladder to heaven. Earth is not convenient, it is good; it is, by God's design, our lawful love. Another toast then.[3]

Think of your favorite food. Steak perhaps. Or Thai green curry. Or ice cream. Or homemade apple pie. God could have just made fuel. He could have made us to be sustained by some kind of savory biscuit. Instead he gave a vast and wonderful array of foods.

The world is more delicious than it needs to be. We have a super-abundance of divine goodness and generosity. God went over the top. We don't need the variety we enjoy, but he gave it to us out of sheer exuberant joy and grace. God's creative joy wasn't only for the beginning of creation, leaving us "eating leftovers." God continues to sustain creation out of joy. "The bloom of yeast lies upon the grape skins year after year because He likes it; $C_6H_{12}O_6=2C_2H_5OH+2CO_2$ is a dependable process because, every September, He says, That was nice; do it again."[4] This means the quality of our food should matter to us. We're to treat food as a gift, not merely as fuel. We're to treat creation as a responsibility entrusted to our care by God to be used for his glory. We should take an interest in where our food comes from: the ingredients in the meal, the care of the livestock, the conditions of the workers, the treatment of the producers.

In his book *Fast Food Nation*, Eric Schlosser describes animals who never see the sun, and who are fattened on grain, pumped with steroids, and slaughtered in factories by workers paid one-third less than forty years ago and receiving minimal benefits.[5] It doesn't have to be like this. Schlosser commends the West Coast burger chain In-N-Out, where the workers are well-paid, with full health benefits, and where food is prepared on the premises from fresh ingredients. Esther and Harry Snyder started the restaurant the same year that McDonald's was started. When their son, Will, a Christian, took over the business, he discreetly introduced Bible references to their packaging.

The best thing you can do for your health is to eat less processed food, which is full of added sugar, salt, and fat—none of which is good for us in large quantities. "When my generation of women walked away from the kitchen," Barbara Kingsolver says, "we were escorted down that path by a profiteering industry that knew a tired, vulnerable marketing target when they saw it. 'Hey, ladies,' it said to us, 'go ahead, get liberated. *We'll* take care of dinner.' They threw open the door and we walked into a nutritional crisis and genuinely toxic food supply."[6] Many of us have structured our busy lives around the availability of processed food, so we may need to change our lifestyles as well as our shopping baskets if we want to enjoy good food in good company. Food is not meant to be "fast." Dietrich Bonhoeffer says:

> The breaking of bread together has a festive quality. In the midst of the working day given to us again and again, it is a reminder that God rested after God's work, and that the Sabbath is the meaning and the goal of the week with its toil. Our life is not only a great deal of trouble and hard work; it is also refreshment and joy in God's goodness. We labour, but God nourishes and sustains us. That is a reason to celebrate. . . . God will not tolerate the unfestive, joyless manner in which we eat our bread with sighs of groaning, with pompous, self-important busyness, or even with shame. Through the daily meal God is calling us to rejoice, to celebrate in the midst of our working day.[7]

Not only did God give us food, he also ordained cooking. Cooking is a central expression of the cultural mandate. God gave this world to us to care for and cultivate. But he also gave it to us to explore and develop. It was God's intention that we take the raw material of his world and use it to create science, culture, agriculture, music, technology, and poetry—all to his glory. Every time you bake a cake, you're fulfilling that creation mandate. Every cake is a reminder of our freedom to create and be creative in the image of the Creator. Every time you place a meal on the table with quiet satisfaction, you're sharing the joy of the Creator at the creation of the world when he declared everything good.

Give Us Each Day Our Daily Bread

In Babylonian creation myths Marduk made man to "establish for his fathers the great food offerings," to bear "food-offerings . . . for their gods."[8] In contrast "God's gift of food is the climax of the six days of creation. . . . Genesis 1 ends . . . with a menu."[9] In pagan myths humanity is made to give food to the gods. In the Bible story God gives food to humanity. Idols demand that we meet their needs. The true God graciously meets our needs.

Eating is an expression of our dependence. God made us in such a way that we need to eat. We're embedded in creation; this means that every time we eat, we're reminded of our dependence on others. Few of us eat food we ourselves have grown and cooked. Even the more self-sufficient among us still rely on other people. Food forces us to live in community, to share, to cooperate, and to trade. In all societies there's a division of labor, which means we work together to provide the food we need. This division of labor frees us from constant hunting and gathering to develop science and art. A humble loaf of bread expresses the mandate God gave humanity to develop agriculture, technology, society, commerce, and culture.

Above all, food expresses our dependence on God. Only God is self-sufficient. We are creatures, and every moment we're sustained by him. Even our rebellion against him is only possible because he holds the fabric of our universe together by his powerful word. Our shouts of defiance against God are only possible with the breath he gives.

Every time we eat, we celebrate again our dependence on God and his faithfulness to his creation. Every time. Food is to be received with gratitude. "Taking the five loaves . . . he gave thanks" (Luke 9:16, NIV).

"Nobody in the ancient world ever took their food for granted."[10] Today it's different. Today we have Walmart. Walmart receives one dollar of every five dollars customers spend on food. If it were a nation, Walmart's economy would be larger than Argentina's. In the UK the equivalent is Tesco. According to Andrew Simms, "there is little, now, that Tesco does not promise in terms of meeting your daily needs." Notice the godlike language. "Not only does Tesco aspire to become the commercial equivalent of the nanny state, providing every product and service imaginable—something that is unhealthy for many reasons—it also aspires to have a store format for every location."[11] Tesco is omnipresent and omnipotent. Walmart is Walmart Jireh, Walmart the Provider. We may direct our prayers to God, but it's Walmart to whom we go for daily bread.

"Give us each day our daily bread" (Luke 11:2–3). That is how Jesus teaches us to pray. We need to pray for our daily bread not because we're worried about where our next meal might come from, but because we're not.

We not only express our dependence on God by feasting, but also by fasting. Just as food points to the goodness of God, so the hunger of fasting reminds us of our need for God. Most of us rarely get hungry before the next intake of food comes along. When we perceive no need, then our self-sovereignty is undisturbed. But fasting brings our need to the fore. Fasting reminds us that we're creatures. We're not self-existent. As the hunger pains bite, we recognize with gratitude and prayer our dependence on creation, on community, and on God.

Fasting reminds us that we depend on God for physical satisfaction, but also for spiritual satisfaction. Our hunger for food heightens our hunger for God. We typically become grumpy when we're hungry. Some of us medicate through food. Our habit when in need is to turn first to food for escape or refuge. Fasting retrains us to turn to God. In Matthew 6:18 Jesus promises a reward to those who fast in secret. What is this reward? It's not a reward that we earn as if fasting were some sort of meritorious act. The reward rather is God himself. John Piper says: "The question is not of earning or meriting or coercing anything from God. The question is: Having tasted the goodness of God in the gospel, how can I maximize my enjoyment of him, when every moment of my life I am tempted to make a god out of his good gifts?"[12]

Learning to turn to God instead of food is a transferable lesson. Fasting trains us to turn to God whenever temptation comes. "If it feels good, do it," our culture says. Or, we might say, "If it tastes good, eat it." We deny ourselves nothing. But a life without self-denial is a flabby life—physically and spiritually. Think about the training regimen of your sporting heroes. Paul urges us to adopt a spiritual training regimen so we're not controlled by our bodily appetites. "I discipline my body and keep it under control . . . ," he says (1 Cor. 9:24–27). Martin Luther said: "Of fasting I say this: it is right to fast frequently in order to subdue and control the body. For when the stomach is full, the body does not serve for preaching, for praying, for studying, or for doing anything else that is good."[13]

One of the dangers of fasting is that some people think abstinence is the epitome of godliness, and they regard food as a distraction from spiritual living. But I suspect most of us face the opposite danger: we've lost much of our ability to appreciate food because we overconsume. We miss the physical joy of being satisfied because we're perpetually satisfied. Fasting is any opportunity to rediscover the joy of simple food received as a gift from God.

Paul warns Timothy of false teachers who "forbid marriage and require abstinence from foods . . ." (1 Tim. 4:3). You're spiritual, these false teachers argued, if you deny your physical appetites for food and sex. The result, however, is that we're separated from God (because we spurn his goodness), from other people (because we're elitist), and from the creation (because we treat it as inferior). Paul calls this teaching demonic (1 Tim. 4:1).

There aren't many in our culture who tell us to refrain from sex. But there are plenty who tell us to refrain from food. Food fads warn against eating certain food types. Some people obsessively count calories or measure their carbohydrate intake. People are always attaching numbers to food, treating it as fuel or medicine or even a kind of poison. Some Christians believe abstinence is the epitome of spirituality.

Paul is clearly not commending gluttony. It's all too possible to overconsume when we look to food for refuge. Food quality and quantity matter. But we must be careful not to lose sight of the fact that food is a divine gift. Food is good. Paul continues: "For everything created by God is good, and nothing is to be rejected if it is received with thanksgiving, for it is made holy by the word of God and prayer" (1 Tim. 4:4–5). We make our food holy when we accept that God's Word declares it good and when we give thanks to God for it in prayer.

We need to rediscover the rhythm of "saying grace" before meals. Perhaps some of us need to discover this for the first time; others may need to refresh what has become a stale habit. What do we express when we say grace?

- Our daily dependence on God as creatures and sinners.
- Our dependence on others as we give thanks for those who grew, processed, bought, and cooked our food.
- The goodness of food, thereby transforming our food from fuel to a gift to be relished.
- Our gratitude to God, thereby reorienting ourselves away from self and back to God.
- Our gratitude for community as we ask God's blessing on our fellowship over the meal.

How important it is to be reminded of these wonderful truths. What a difference they make to our enjoyment of God and food and each other. If only we had three opportunities each day to remember and enact these truths!

God set a table so we could eat in his presence. This is the heart of what it means to be human. It involves physicality. God didn't create us for mere mental contemplation, but for a shared meal. But neither is the meal everything. "God has put us together in such a way that our hunger for the gift of food is designed to lead us to the Giver."[14] "Man does not live by bread alone, but man lives by every word that comes from the mouth of the LORD" (Deut. 8:3).

4

Meals as Enacted Mission

Luke 14

To celebrate the Kurdish New Year, one of our missional communities threw a party. We provided kebabs and live music. Over one hundred Kurds from across the city converged on the party. Our main worry was whether the floor would hold. Standing in the basement, we could see that the Kurdish men dancing in sync above was causing the floor to flex by at least an inch. The floor held, and the evening ended with my friend Samuel telling everyone we'd put on this party to express God's love for Kurds.

My wife invited a work colleague over one Saturday evening to join our family takeout night. We had a couple of Christian friends from one of our sister churches staying with us at that time. We all shared a curry and watched the UK version of *American Idol.* "Your home was a place of refuge," the colleague wrote in a text message the next day. A few weeks later she started reading the Bible with my wife and me.

Each month one of our missional communities hosts a curry night for Pakistani men. A dozen or so come to enjoy homemade curry and conversation. That's it. There's not much to add. Except that relationships are growing and gospel opportunities are increasing. More recently they've started a similar evening for Pakistani women.

Every year a street is closed to traffic and becomes the venue for a neighborhood party with live music, games, competitions, and barbequed food. Three or four families in our missional communities are the prime movers behind urban street parties.

In a community hall underneath the Sheffield United soccer stadium, more than a hundred people of all nationalities gathered. Our church had paid a Pakistani friend to make biryani curry, and church members provided desserts. At a couple of points in the meal we told stories of meals—the story of the woman who washed the feet of Jesus in Luke 7 and the story of the prodigal son in Luke 15.

One night Guy and Belinda, members of our missional community, held a barbeque—two Christian couples and two unbelieving couples enjoyed the homemade hamburgers, marinated chicken, potato salad, and a family-recipe relish. Plus a plum cake made by our Polish friend. Conversations about politics, soccer, work, food (of course), and faith flowed.

One of the churches in our network is reaching Bengalis. People from the church buy ingredients from a local Asian foodstore, go home, and make a recipe from a Bengali cookbook. At closing time they take their efforts to the shopkeeper. They eat at the back of the shop and talk about the Bible and Islam. On Sundays they bake bread with friends from the local residents' association and teach their Bengali neighbors to cook English food while being shown how to cook Asian food.

Recently we invited a new couple in our neighborhood over for a meal, along with a young couple from our church. We put all the food on the dining room table and invited people to help themselves. Then we took our plates out to eat under the apple tree in our garden. "How do you know each other?" they asked us. "We belong to the same church." "Which church is that?" "It's a church that meets in a home down the road." "In a home? Why's that?" . . .

One of our missional communities is reaching Pakistanis. It organized a picnic in the countryside for one particular Pakistani family, but others started to get invited. In the end forty people made their way by car and train to the picnic spot, where they ended up sharing food, playing games, and building relationships.

These are all forms of mission Jesus would recognize. They are the kinds of events he might have attended. The Son of Man came eating and drinking.

But they are also ways of doing mission that you could do. In one sense none of these meals is anything special. They don't require any special training or a course in apologetics or a grasp of the latest missiological jargon. When you combine a passion for Jesus with shared meals, you create potent gospel opportunities.

Members of our missional community started visiting a Kurdish café. As they got to know more Kurds, they were invited to the "casino" upstairs. What den of iniquity was this? they wondered. It turned out to be a games room with backgammon, sweet black tea, Kurdish television, and a thick blanket of cigarette smoke. Two years later a group of Kurds were meeting each week to study the Bible.

Two doors down from the Kurdish café is a church-run café. It never seems to have more than one or two people. Running a café may be a great missional project in your context, especially in neighborhoods where there are few other meeting places. But it's hard work. It requires significant amounts of money and time. Attending an existing café or bar requires no special effort. Jesus didn't open a café. He accepted invitations.

What are some of the things you associate with a party? What do most people today associate with church? How can we make church feel more like a party?

Luke 14:1–24

One Sabbath, when he went to dine at the house of a ruler of the Pharisees, they were watching him carefully. And behold, there was a man before him who had dropsy. And Jesus responded to the lawyers and Pharisees, saying, "Is it lawful to heal on the Sabbath, or not?" But they remained silent. Then he took him and healed him and sent him away. And he said to them, "Which of you, having a son or an ox that has fallen into a well on a Sabbath day, will not immediately pull him out?" And they could not reply to these things.

Now he told a parable to those who were invited, when he noticed how they chose the places of honor, saying to them, "When you are invited by someone to a wedding feast, do not sit down in a place of honor, lest someone more distinguished than you be invited by him, and he who invited you both will come and say to you, 'Give your place to this person,' and then you will begin with shame to take the lowest place. But when you are invited, go and sit in the lowest place, so that when your host comes he may say to you, 'Friend, move up higher.' Then you will be honored in the presence of all who sit at table with you. For everyone who exalts himself will be humbled, and he who humbles himself will be exalted."

He said also to the man who had invited him, "When you give a dinner or a banquet, do not invite your friends or your brothers or your relatives or rich neighbors, lest they also invite you in return and you be repaid. But when you give a feast, invite the poor, the crippled, the lame, the blind, and you will be blessed, because they cannot repay you. You will be repaid at the resurrection of the just."

When one of those who reclined at table with him heard these things, he said to him, "Blessed is everyone who will eat bread in the kingdom of God!" But he said to him, "A man once gave a great banquet and invited many. And at the time for the banquet he sent his servant to say to those who had been invited, 'Come, for everything is now ready.' But they all alike began to make excuses. The first said to him, 'I have bought a field, and I must go out and see it. Please have me excused.' And another said, 'I have bought five yoke of oxen, and I go to examine them. Please have me excused.' And another said, 'I have married a wife, and therefore I cannot come.' So the servant came and reported these things to his master. Then the master of the house became angry and said to his servant, 'Go out quickly to the streets and lanes of the city, and bring in the poor and crippled and blind and lame.' And the servant said, 'Sir, what you commanded has been done, and still there is room.' And the master said to the servant, 'Go out to the highways and hedges and compel people to come in, that my house may be filled. For I tell you, none of those men who were invited shall taste my banquet.'"

All the themes we have met so far are again present in this meal.

We see again God's grace to us. We're the poor, the blind, the crippled, and the lame, urged inside to join God's great banquet. We are:

- the spiritually poor—with nothing to offer for our salvation;
- the spiritually crippled—made powerless by sin;
- the spiritually blind—unable to see the truth about Jesus;
- the spiritually lame—unable to come to God on our own.

Extending Leviticus 21:17-23, most Jewish authorities said no one who was blind, crippled, or lame could enter the temple. How amazing it was, then, that after Jesus cleansed the temple, "the blind and the lame came to him in the temple, and he healed them" (Matt. 21:14). Documents from Qumran show that the Essenes sect interpreted Leviticus 21 to mean that the poor, the blind, the crippled, and the lame wouldn't participate in the messianic banquet.[1] How significant, then, that in Jesus's message, they're the very ones who are included.

We also see again that God's grace is the foundation for Christian community. In Luke 14:12 Jesus talks about giving "a dinner or a banquet." In verse 16 the man who prepares a banquet represents God, who invites us to a great banquet. Our parties are to be a reflection—albeit a pale reflection—of God's great banquet.

We see again the way religious people reject God's grace (Luke 14:16–24). A double invitation was common in traditional Middle Eastern culture. You invited guests and decided what animals to butcher in light of the responses you received. A second invitation was sent out, perhaps the following day, when everything was ready: "Come, for everything is now ready" (v. 17). The subsequent excuses in this story are lame, if not downright insulting. No one would buy land or oxen without inspecting them first, and the banquet would have been held after the close of the working day. The marriage can't have been recent, otherwise the wedding banquet and this one would have clashed (and the hosts would have planned for that not to happen). Moreover, to suggest you were busy with your wife would have been rude in a culture that was extremely discreet about women and sex.[2] Jesus's point is clear. The long-awaited messianic banquet is approaching (see Luke 5:34). "Come, for everything is now ready" (Luke 14:17). But the invited guests (like the religious leaders) reject the banquet and insult the host. So the invitation goes out to the outcasts of Israel and then out still further to the Gentiles in the highways and hedges. Here people have to be compelled to come, because they can hardly believe they've been invited. The closing words of this story are "my banquet." I can't help but imagine a subtle emphasis on the word "my" as Jesus speaks, so the words of the master in the story become the words of the storyteller. The banquet of the Messiah is ready. Are you really going to refuse your invitation?

We also see the worlds of grace and religion colliding in the healing of the man with dropsy. Here is one of the "crippled." Jesus's later inclusion of the crippled in verses 13 and 21 suggests that he intends his exhortation in verses 12–14 and the parable of the banquet to be a commentary on this healing event. Religion has nothing to offer this crippled man, but Jesus brings healing. The Pharisees hadn't experienced grace or recognized their own need. As a result they had no grace for the needy. They had nothing to offer and nothing to say (vv. 4, 6).

If you want to see a religious person's vision of life, then show up at one of their meals. There's no restoration on the Sabbath. There's jockeying for position. The poor are excluded. The religious think their meals maintain the purity of Israel. But Jesus says they're the threat to the people of God. It's an ugly vision and not at all inviting.

Meals can be a visual representation of our hearts. If our hearts are concerned for position, honor, status, or approval, then that will be reflected in our dining etiquette. Consider how your meals express your vision for life. Think about who's invited, how they're served, what you hope to achieve, and the layout of your home. Do they express the vision of the kingdom of God?

Eating Together as Enacted Mission

What's new in the story of the great banquet is the exhortation to invite outsiders to our meals. Jesus told this story while dining at a Pharisee's house. We get an idea of this host's guest list from verse 3: "Jesus responded to the lawyers and Pharisees. . . ." The host's guests were people like him. But it wasn't just the Jewish world where you ate with your own: "Central to the political stability of the Empire was the ethics of reciprocity, a gift-and-obligation system that tied every person, from the emperor in Rome to the child in the most distant province, into an intricate web of social relations. . . . Expectations of reciprocity were naturally extended to the table."[3] Giving food to the poor was okay. But you gave them food at your back door. You never invited them in. That meant contamination. Scott Bartchy writes: "Beyond the household, people generally preferred to eat with persons from their own social class."[4] It's not so very different today. We still like to eat with people like us.

But Jesus says, "When you give a dinner or a banquet, do not invite your friends or your brothers or your relatives or your rich neighbors, lest they also invite you in return and you be repaid. But when you give a feast, invite the poor, the crippled, the lame, the blind, and you will be blessed, because they cannot repay you. For you will be repaid at the resurrection of the just" (vv. 12–14). The table fellowship of Jesus, with its ethic of grace rather than reciprocity, was creating a new countercultural society in the midst of the Empire. "The behaviors Jesus demands would collapse the distance between rich and poor, insider and outsider."[5]

Audit the activities of your church. How many offer some kind of reciprocal payback? Is your youth program designed to reach lost young people in your neighborhood or to provide a safe haven for church kids? Are your home groups doing adventurous mission together or offering a cozy support group?

Luke repeats the poor, the crippled, the blind, and the lame in verses 13 and 21. These four examples represent the marginalized, powerless, and vulnerable as a whole. They're the "orphans and widows" of James 1:27 and the "tax collectors and sinners" of Luke 15:1. Our attitude to the marginalized is to be shaped by our experience of God's grace to us. God welcomes us to his party, and so we're to welcome the poor. The kind of fasting that God desires is "to share your bread with the hungry and bring the homeless poor into your house" (Isa. 58:7).

We're called to follow Christ into a broken world. Simply writing a check keeps the poor at a distance. But Jesus was the *friend* of sinners. As we learned in chapter 2, to invite someone for a meal in Jesus's time was an expression of identification. That's why Jesus's habit of eating with tax collectors and sinners was so scandalous. He was saying, "These are my sort of people." Christine Pohl says:

> Often we maintain significant boundaries when offering help to persons in need. Many churches prepare and serve meals to hungry neighbors, but few church members find it easy to sit and eat with those who need the meal. When people are very different from ourselves, we often find it more comfortable to cook and clean for them than to share in a meal and conversation. We are familiar with roles as helpers but are less certain about being equals eating together. Many of us struggle with simply being present with people in need; our helping roles give definition to the relationship but they also keep it decidedly hierarchical.[6]

We think we're enacting grace if we provide for the poor. But we're only halfway there. We've missed the social dynamics. What we communicate is that we're able and you're unable. "I can do something for you, but you can do nothing for me. I'm superior to you." We cloak our superiority in compassion, but superiority cloaked in compassion is patronizing.

Think how different the dynamic is when we sit and eat with someone. We meet as equals. We share together. We affirm one another and enjoy one another. A woman once told me: "I know people do a lot to help me. But what I want is for someone to be my friend." People don't want to be projects. The poor need a welcome to replace their marginalization, inclusion to replace their exclusion, a place where they matter to replace their powerlessness. They need community. They need the Christian community.[7]

If you tell someone he's a sinner who needs God while you're handing him a cup of soup, then he'll hear you saying he's a loser who should become like you. But when you eat together as friends and you tell him what a messed up person you are, then you can tell him about sin and grace. Jim Petersen writes: "I know of no more effective environment for initiating evangelism than a dinner at home or in a quiet restaurant."[8]

Consider Jesus. Yes, he adopted the attitude of slave when he washed the disciples' feet. But think, too, how often he accepts service. He accepts hospitality from Levi (Luke 5). He lets the woman at Simon's house wash his feet (Luke 7). He asks for water from the woman in Samaria (John 4). He's not just the helper of sinners, still less their project worker. He's the friends of sinners, who came eating and drinking.

Philip Yancey begins his book *What's So Amazing about Grace?* with the story of a prostitute in Chicago who is asked if she'd ever thought of going to a church for help. "Church!" she cries. "Why would I ever go there? I was already feeling terrible about myself. They'd just make me feel worse."[9]

Prostitutes loved sharing a meal with Jesus (Luke 15:1–2). They avoid the church he founded like the plague. Something has gone wrong:

> Jesus's teaching consistently attracted the irreligious while offending the Bible-believing, religious people of his day. However, in the main, our churches today do not have this effect. The kind of outsiders Jesus attracted are not attracted to contemporary churches, even our most avant-garde ones. We tend to draw conservative, buttoned-down, moralistic people. The licentious and liberated or the broken and marginal avoid church. That can only mean one thing. If the preaching of our ministers and the practice of our parishioners do not have the same effect on people that Jesus had, then we must not be declaring the same message that Jesus did.[10]

The Great Reversal

The maneuvering for places of honor in Luke 14:7–11 was normal behavior. Guests' standing in society dictated where they sat, so allocating seats was a fraught process.[11] But what are we to make of Jesus's advice to take a lower position so you would get moved up? Is this just a bit of homely wisdom or advice on social etiquette? I think not. The punch line is verse 11: "For everyone who exalts himself will be humbled, and he who humbles himself will be exalted." It echoes Luke 1:52–53, where Mary sings: "He has brought down the mighty from their thrones and exalted those of humble estate; he has filled the hungry with good things, and the rich he has sent away empty."

In the kingdom of God the world's ordering of things will be turned on its head. God's choice of poor, insignificant Mary is a sign of what's coming. There will be a reversal of status. Luke's message is: when God reverses the worldly order of things, make sure you're on the underside. Verses 12–14 are about a meal swap: invite the marginalized, just as God invites you (who were once marginalized from him) to his resurrection feast. Verses 7–11 are about a position swap: instead of jockeying for status, humble yourself and God will honor you at the resurrection. "Because the sharing of food is a 'delicate barometer' of social relations, when Jesus subverts conventional mealtime practices relating to seating arrangements and invitations, he is doing more than offering sage counsel for his table companions. Rather, he is toppling the familiar world of the ancient Mediterranean, overturning its socially constructed reality and replacing it with what must have been regarded as a scandalous alternative."[12]

It's time to take a step back and ask why Luke wrote his Gospel. He opens by saying: "It seemed good to me also, having followed all things closely for some time past, to write an orderly account for you, most excellent Theophilus, that you may have certainty concerning the things you have been taught" (1:3–4).

What has Theophilus been taught, and how does Luke's account bring certainty? If Theophilus has been taught just the story of the life of Jesus, then it's difficult to see how Luke's account might add certainty. I suggest that Theophilus has been taught that a day is coming when the first shall be last and the last shall be first. He's been taught that God has an eternal banquet to which sinners are invited, but from which the self-righteous and the self-important are excluded.

Just before the meal of Luke 14, Luke reminds us of this great reversal, again with meals at the fore. Judgment is described as hospitality refused: "When once the master of the house has risen and shut the door, and you begin to stand outside and to knock at the door, saying, 'Lord, open to us,' then he will answer you, 'I do not know where you come from'" (Luke 13:25). Having shared a meal with Jesus (as the Pharisees did in Luke 14) will not be enough (13:26–27). Jesus longed to gather the children of Jerusalem, but they wouldn't come (13:34). This is the story the parable of the great banquet will retell in chapter 14. Now the participants of the messianic banquet will be drawn from across the world. "People will come from east and west, and from north and south, and recline at table in the kingdom of God" (13:29). The conclusion is this: "Behold, some are last who will be first, and some are first who will be last" (13:30). A great reversal is coming.

Luke's account of Jesus can give Theophilus certainty of the things he has been taught because it demonstrates that Jesus's ministry—and above all his table fellowship—is a foretaste of the great reversal. Jesus welcomes sinners and eats with them, just as God will do in his eternal banquet. He humbles the self-righteous and self-important, but welcomes the humble and marginalized. Jesus's ministry is a picture of the great reversal on the final day. The makeup of the Christian community is a powerful testimony to the rich and powerful.

It's common to hear that we need to reach the cultural elite and opinion-formers if we want to transform the culture. No doubt there's something in this. But the danger is that if we adapt to reach the rich and powerful on their terms, then nothing changes. Luke's alternative strategy for reaching people like the "most excellent" Theophilus is to point to the table fellowship of Jesus. We reach the rich by reaching the poor. Only in this way will we challenge the value system of the elite and embody God's grace (1 Cor. 1:26–31).

If there is going to be a day of reversal, then Theophilus needs to align himself with the marginalized, poor, and persecuted community of Jesus. Scott Bartchy comments: "Luke's emphasis was probably 'hard bread' for the elite Christians among his readers. For participation in such a socially inclusive community might well have cut them off from their prior social networks on which their status depended."[13] That's the significance of verses 7–11. Make sure you're lowly, because one day the lowly will be exalted. Make sure you're with the outsiders, because one day the outsiders will be insiders. Throughout Luke's Gospel one's attitude to the poor is the touchstone of genuine discipleship.

The call to believe the message of this coming reversal is the reason why confidence in the Word of God is also such an important theme in Luke's Gospel.[14] Luke wants Theophilus to trust God's word about the future. Luke 11 tell us: "A woman in the crowd raised her voice and said to him, 'Blessed is the womb that bore you, and the breasts at which you nursed!' But he said, 'Blessed rather are those who hear the word of God and keep it!'" (vv. 27–28).

Luke's plea for people to believe the message of the great reversal also explains another significant theme in his Gospel: the threat posed by possessions. This is what threatens to stop people like "most excellent" Theophilus from committing themselves to Christ's community. "No servant can serve two masters, for either he will hate the one and love the other, or he will be devoted to the one and despise the other. You cannot serve God and money" (Luke 16:13). In the parable of the great banquet, people refuse their invitations because they're distracted by the things of this world (14:18–20). In the parable of the sower, the seed sown among thorns represents people who fail to produce a crop because "they are choked by the cares and riches and pleasures of life" (8:14). Jesus warns a crowd of listeners: "Be on your guard against all covetousness, for one's life does not consist in the abundance of his possessions" (12:15) before telling a parable of a farmer who has a bumper crop, but is not rich toward God (12:16–21). Jesus "lifted up his eyes on his disciples, and said: 'Blessed are you who are poor, for yours is the kingdom of God. . . . But woe to you who are rich, for you have received your consolation" (6:20, 24). The rich young ruler of Luke 18 leaves Jesus sad, because he loves his possessions, prompting Jesus to say: "How difficult it is for those who have wealth to enter the kingdom of God! For it is easier for a camel to go through the eye of a needle than for a rich person to enter the kingdom of God" (18:24–25).

Shortly after his encounter with this rich young man, Jesus meets another rich man and invites himself over for a meal (Luke 19:1–

10). Zacchaeus clearly loved money, because he'd sacrificed social acceptance to gain it and made himself an enemy of God. That's a high price to pay. Yet after his encounter with Jesus, Zacchaeus is a changed man.[15] Unlike the respectable rich man in Luke 18 whose possessions prevent him following Jesus, Zacchaeus expresses his repentance by declaring that he'll give away half his wealth and repay fourfold whomever he's cheated. The grace of God embodied in the meal with Jesus liberates Zacchaeus from his enslaving greed. That's the pattern Luke invites us to follow.

Meals enact mission. But they enact mission because they enact grace. We don't know what Zacchaeus already knew or what Jesus might have said over the meal. But we know the invitation of Jesus scandalized the crowd (v. 7)—this "small" man was a *persona non grata* (literally, a person without grace) in their eyes. This invitation expressed God's grace, and God's grace transformed Zacchaeus's heart.

The film *Babette's Feast* tells the story of an eighteenth-century Christian community in Denmark that has lost its way, becoming joyless and legalistic. Babette is a refugee from Paris who comes to live with two sisters. For twelve years she serves as their housekeeper, learning how to prepare their humble food. Then she wins ten thousand francs. (Each year a friend has renewed her Paris lottery ticket, and this year her number has come up.) Babette asks if she can prepare a banquet for the community. She serves up course after course of the most exquisite food, climaxing in a dish of baby quail. A visiting general exclaims he has only ever tasted food like this at the famous Café Anglais in Paris. As the meal unfolds, the community rediscovers joy. Feuds are ended. Sin is confessed. The evening ends with the community hand-in-hand around the village fountain singing the old songs of faith. Meanwhile the two sisters find Babette in the chaos of the kitchen. With a faraway look in her eyes she says, "I was once cook at the Café Anglais." "We will all remember this evening," the sisters say, "when you have gone back to Paris." But Babette will not be returning to Paris. She has spent all the ten thousand francs on the feast. A lavish meal has brought transformation to a joyless community because it embodied grace.[16]

Mission through Meals

Jesus didn't run projects, establish ministries, create programs, or put on events. He ate meals. If you routinely share meals and you have a passion for Jesus, then you'll be doing mission. It's not that meals save people. People are saved through the gospel message. But meals will create natural opportunities to share that message in a context that resonates powerfully with what you're saying.

Hospitality has always been integral to the story of God's people. Abraham set the agenda when he offered three strangers water for their feet and food for their bodies. In so doing he entertained God himself and received afresh the promise (Gen. 18:1–18). God was Israel's host in the Promised Land (Ps. 39:12; Lev. 25:23), and that would later shape Israel's behavior. A welcome to strangers and provision for the needy were written into the law of Moses. Rahab is saved because of her faith expressed through hospitality (Joshua 2; James 2:22–25).

Hospitality continues to be integral to Christian conduct in the new covenant: "Contribute to the needs of the saints and seek to show hospitality" (Rom. 12:13); "Show hospitality to one another without grumbling" (1 Pet. 4:9; see 1 Tim. 5:10); "Whoever receives you receives me, and whoever receives me receives him who sent me" (Matt. 10:40; see 25:35–40); "Do not neglect to show hospitality to strangers, for thereby some have entertained angels unawares" (Heb. 13:2).

In Acts 10 God told Peter in a dream to eat from a collection of unclean food. It's a key moment in the mission of the early church, for its prepares Peter to take the gospel to Gentiles for the first time. Peter says to those Gentiles: "You yourselves know how unlawful it is for a Jew to associate with or to visit anyone of another nation, but God has shown me that I should not call any person common or unclean. So when I was sent for, I came without objection . . ." (Acts 10:28–29). Mission to the nations begins with a new understanding of hospitality.

Hospitality has continued to be integral to the church's mission, at times being its primary expression. The Rule of St. Benedict, written around 540, says, "All guests who present themselves are to be welcomed as Christ, for he himself will say: 'I was a stranger and you welcomed me.'" Monasticism, for all its faults, got this right: it expressed mission through hospitality to rich and poor alike. "Only monasticism," Richard Niebuhr claimed, "saved the medieval church from acquiescence, petrifaction, and the loss of its vision and truly revolutionary character."[17] Missiologist David Bosch writes: "For upwards of seven hundred years . . . the monastery was notably the center of culture and civilization, but also of mission. In the midst of a world ruled by love of self, the monastic communities were a visible sign and preliminary realization of a world ruled by the love of God."[18] Monasteries weren't necessarily founded for mission, but their occupants' piety, hard work, learning, tenacity, and hospitality had a profound impact on the common people. "Each monastery was a vast complex of buildings, churches, workshops, stores, and almshouses—a hive of activity for the benefit of the entire surrounding community. The citizens of the heavenly city were actively seeking the peace and good order of the earthly city."[19]

Meals continue to be integral to the task of mission. Theologian and chef Simon Carey Holt says:

> It's good to be reminded that the table is a very ordinary place, a place so routine and everyday it's easily overlooked as a place of ministry. And this business of hospitality that lies at the heart of Christian mission, it's a very ordinary thing; it's not rocket science nor is it terribly glamorous. Yet it is the very ordinariness of the table and of the ministry we exercise there that renders these elements of

Christian life so important to the mission of the church. . . . Most
of what you do as a community of hospitality will go unnoticed and
unrecognized. At base, hospitality is about providing a space for God's
Spirit to move. Setting a table, cooking a meal, washing the dishes is
the ministry of facilitation: providing a context in which people feel
loved and welcome and where God's Spirit can be at work in their
lives. Hospitality is a very ordinary business, but in its ordinariness
is its real worth.[20]

Elsewhere Holt says: "Whatever it looks like, your own table is a
sacred place and one just as implicated by the lavish nature of God's
grace as any other."[21]

Meals bring mission into the ordinary. But that's where most
people are—living in the ordinary. That's where we need to go
to reach them. We too readily think of mission as extraordinary.
Perhaps that's because we find it awkward to talk about Jesus outside a church gathering. Perhaps it's because we think God moves
through the spectacular rather than the witness of people like us.
Perhaps it's because we want to outsource mission to the professionals, so we invite people to guest services where an "expert" can
do mission for us. But most people live in the ordinary, and most
people will be reached by ordinary people. Even those who attend
a special event will, for the most part, have first been befriended
by a Christian. "For those looking to connect with people in the
local community it isn't that hard if you really want to. Just invite
people round, let them know they can go home if they need to and
then enjoy a meal together. You're going to eat anyway, so why not
do it with others!"[22]

Jesus's command to invite the poor for dinner violates our notions
of distance and detachment. Mission as hospitality undermines the
professionalization of ministry. Mission isn't something I can clock
out from at the end of the day. The hospitality to which Jesus calls us
can't be institutionalized in programs and projects. Jesus challenges
us to take mission home. It may be a surprise, given my emphasis

on meals, but I loathe church lunches—those potluck suppers in draughty church halls. They're institutionalized hospitality. Don't start a hospitality ministry in your church: open your home.

Much is said of engaging with culture—much that's right and helpful. But we must never let engaging culture eclipse engaging with people. People are infinitely variable and rarely susceptible to our sociological categories. If you want to understand a person's worldview, don't read a book. Talk to them, hang out with them, eat with them.

People often complain that they lack time for mission. But we all have to eat. Three meals a day, seven days a week. That's twenty-one opportunities for mission and community without adding anything to your schedule. You could meet up with another Christian for breakfast on the way to work—read the Bible together, offer accountability, pray for one another. You could meet up with colleagues at lunchtime. Put down this book and chat to the person across the table from you in the cafeteria. You could invite your neighbors over for a meal. Better still, invite them over with another family from church. That way you get to do mission and community at the same time; plus your unbelieving neighbors will get to see the way the gospel impacts our relationships as Christians (John 13:34–35; 17:20–21). You could invite someone who lives alone to share your family meal and follow it with board games, giving your children an opportunity to serve others through their welcome. Francis Schaeffer says:

> Don't start with a big program. Don't suddenly think you can add to your church budget and begin. Start personally and start in your home. I dare you. I dare you in the name of Jesus Christ. Do what I am going to suggest. Begin by opening your home for community. . . . You don't need a big program. You don't have to convince your session or board. All you have to do is open your home and begin. And there is no place in God's world where there are no people who will come and share a home as long as it is a real home.[23]

Join in with the cultural events in your neighborhood. The chances are food will be involved somewhere, because food is such a powerful bond. Look for opportunities to reinterpret what is happening in biblical categories. In Acts 14 Paul addresses the people of Lystra. They want to worship him and Barnabas as gods because the two healed a crippled man. Paul calls on them to turn from idolatry, and then says that God "did not leave himself without witness, for he did good by giving you rains from heaven and fruitful seasons, satisfying your hearts with food and gladness" (Acts 14:17). How many evangelistic messages have you heard along these lines? "[God] provides you with plenty of food and fills your hearts with joy" (NIV). So let's give thanks to him rather than worshiping "vain things" (v. 15). We should engage in party evangelism.

I wonder what kind of reputation Christians have in your neighborhood. We should have a reputation for throwing the best parties. It's not hard to find an excuse to throw a party:

- personal occasions: birthdays, anniversaries, new jobs, exams, house warmings
- sporting occasions: the Super Bowl, the World Series, the soccer World Cup
- seasonal occasions: the Fourth of July, Thanksgiving, Christmas, New Year
- cultural occasions: Mexican food theme night, the *American Idol* final

There are reasons enough to have a party every week.

Parties, of course, are not enough. They create a great platform for gospel opportunities. But they must be accompanied by a passion for people and a passion for Jesus. You don't have to give a little sermon—just be attentive to people and open about your faith.

Excuses for Not Showing Hospitality

What stops us from being hospitable, when the Bible clearly expects it of God's people?

Too Scary

When we invite people into our homes, we're putting ourselves on display. How will they evaluate our cooking, cleaning, decor, or parenting? Craving other people's approval or fearing their censure is what the Bible calls "the fear of man." The Bible's antidote is "the fear of the LORD." When God's opinion is what matters most—the God who smiles on us in his grace—then we're liberated to serve others out of love, rather than to gain their good opinion.[24]

Take cleaning the house before guests arrive. If your aim is to impress, then you'll feel compelled to clean. If your aim is to love, then the compulsion isn't there. You may clean as an act of love, but love may conclude that an hour with the children is more important. Both very dirty houses and very tidy houses make me feel uncomfortable. In the case of very tidy homes, I'm always afraid I'm going to pollute the show-home perfection. If your house is somewhere in between, then I'll feel at home!

Elaborate dinner parties can easily become hospitality-as-performance. They promise intimacy, but can in fact maintain distance through formality. The focus of entertaining is impressing others; the focus of true hospitality is serving others. People sometimes say that blue-collar people don't do hospitality. In fact what people are saying is that they don't do formal dinner parties. While professionals invite you over next week, blue-collar people invite you over now. If someone just drops by, he very well might end up staying for dinner. You'll need to fit in with the rhythms of the people you're serving.

Sharing food doesn't necessarily require hosting. Jesus was a guest more often than he was a host. If your circumstances make hosting people in your home difficult, you can still find ways to eat with others. Or you could invite someone out for a cup of coffee.

Sometimes I've told visitors to go home so my wife could get some rest. If you're driven in ministry to prove yourself, then you'll find it hard to say no when you should. But we don't need to prove ourselves. We're justified by the finished work of Christ. All the proving has been done by him. We serve from freedom. Hospitality only becomes a burden when we're driven to prove ourselves or impress others.

Remember, too, that we're witnesses to grace, not to good works and certainly not to good catering. Jim Petersen tells the story of his friend Mario, with whom he had studied the Bible for four years before Mario became a Christian. The Bible studies reflected the fact that Mario was a Marxist intellectual who'd read all the leading Western philosophers. A couple of years after his conversion, Jim and Mario were reminiscing: "Do you know what it really was that made me decide to become a Christian?" Mario asked. Petersen thought of all their Bible studies and philosophical discussions. Mario's reply took him by surprise. "Remember that first time I stopped by your house? We were on our way someplace together, and I had a bowl of soup with you and your family. As I sat there observing you, your wife, and your children, and how you related to each other, I asked myself, 'When will I have a relationship like this with my fiancée?' When I realized that the answer was 'never,' I concluded I had to become a Christian for the sake of my own survival."[25] Petersen did remember the occasion. He remembered his children behaving badly and his frustration at having to correct them in front of Mario. Yet Mario saw the grace of Christ binding that family together. Petersen comments:

> Our family was unaware of its influence on Mario, God had done this work through our family without our knowing it. . . . We tend to see the weaknesses and incongruities in our lives, and our reaction is

to recoil at the thought of letting outsiders get close enough to see us as we really are. Even if our assessment is accurate, it is my observation that any Christian who is sincerely seeking to walk with God, in spite of all his flaws, is reflecting something of Christ.[26]

Too Costly

Food costs money. Hospitality takes time. Things get broken. There are risks. But our meals don't have to be elaborate and the house doesn't have to be spotless. (Although having a feast from time to time is a great way of celebrating God's lavish generosity.) But never despise the power of inviting people to share a family meal. Plenty of people feel more comfortable in the chaos of family meals than the formality of a dinner party. If you're single, it might be a challenge to provide a meal for a family: you might not be used to large-scale catering, your home might not be big enough, and you probably don't have any toys. But be creative. You could invite a family over for cake or take them out for a picnic.

Above all remember the cost of the messianic banquet: the blood of Jesus. The cross is our motive and our model.[26]

Too Busy

Perhaps you'd love to offer more hospitality, but when? Your life already feels full. When you do have a spare evening, all you're fit for is to slump on the sofa.

For busy people, hospitality requires a bit of planning. You may need to set aside an evening or two a week or regularly invite people over for Saturday breakfast. Maybe we need to downsize our church programs. We may be so busy "doing church" that we have no time to "be church," still less to share our lives with unbelievers.

If guests offer to help, then take them up on their offer. Your aim is to love, not impress. Jesus himself was the recipient of hospitality more often than he provided it. Letting others serve us creates a relationship of equality and intimacy. It also means the clearing up won't be waiting for you the next morning!

Above all examine your heart. God didn't make a mistake when he spun the world into being, making twenty-four-hour days instead of twenty-five-hour ones. He expects you to serve him and glorify him in those twenty-four hours. But he doesn't expect you to do twenty-five hours' work in a day. The person responsible for your busyness is you. We're too busy because we're trying to do more than God expects.

- You may be too busy because you're insecure and need to control life. But God is great and cares for you as a sovereign heavenly Father.
- You may be too busy because you fear other people, and so you can't say no. But God is glorious, and his opinion is the one that matters.
- You may be too busy because you're filling your life with activity in a desperate attempt to find satisfaction. But God is good, and the true source of joy.
- You may be too busy because you're trying to prove yourself through your work or ministry. But God is gracious and justifies you freely through Christ's finished work.

You'll never create time for people until you address the issues in your heart and find rest in God's greatness, glory, goodness, and grace.[27]

*

My friend Jeff Vanderstelt, the founder of Soma Communities in the state of Washington, describes the missional approach of him and his wife, Jayne:

> When we first arrived and got settled into our neighborhood, we had a house warming party and invited our friends and neighbors over for a party with good food and drink. We were very intentional to ask

them about themselves, how long they'd been in the neighborhood and general questions about their life. Each time, we were careful to listen well looking for the opportunity to be a blessing to them with what God has given us.

Eventually, Soma began using the first Sunday of the month to do "scattered gatherings" in our neighborhoods instead of gathering in a building together. We trained the church in Hospitality and encouraged our people to open their homes on Sunday mornings for a brunch and invite neighbors to join them. Each of us served as host and provided some main dishes (not just some cheap donuts). Surprisingly, a majority of our neighbors attended (most were not a part of a church). And once again, we asked questions, listened and got to know our neighbors better. One of our goals was to get to know the stories of our neighbors as well as our neighborhood, always looking for an opportunity to be a display of God's grace to our neighbors by the way we hosted and served and eventually through acts of grace according to their needs.

We realized that we needed regularity to this kind of activity so during the Spring and Summer we started doing a BBQ/party every Friday night. The regularity was a key to making this happen. (Too many settle for doing a party a couple times a year . . . this will not do it . . . there needs to be consistency to your hospitality). Eventually, everyone in the neighborhood had joined us and there was a genuine sense of connection and warmth between us relationally. Over time, others volunteered to host the parties so that our neighborhood started sharing the responsibility.

All of this would have been good neighborly activity, but not enough all by itself. It led to us getting to know the felt and real needs of our neighbors. We eventually started working on our neighbor Nicki's home together since her home had fallen apart after the passing of her husband 15 years prior. During our times of serving together, we would often look for opportunities to share the Gospel reason for why we were serving. Most often, after serving we would invite people over for dinner and the conversations continued.

Our home became known as the house where you could find a party or a place to rest, converse, share a struggle or receive some prayer. We let people know that we had an open door policy—if you wanted to stop by and visit or join us for dinner, you were always welcome. This led to people stopping over after a bad day, losing a job, looking for advice on child rearing or crying over a broken relationship. If we needed to be alone for a particular reason, we would politely make that known, but many times the Spirit prompted us to set aside our own interests and pray for strength to love our neighbors when it wasn't always convenient for us. . . .

We have found that the mess and the difficulty of loving hospitality done in the power of the Gospel is one of the most powerful witnesses we've had to our neighborhood.[28]

5

Meals as Enacted Salvation

Luke 22

Baked potatoes, salad, beans, tuna salad, bread, wine. About a dozen or so of us are squeezed round the table. People are laughing, sharing news, and passing around the food. Then Guy calls for quiet. He asks Wendy to thank God for all that the bread and wine represent. He reminds us of the words of Jesus at the Last Supper. Matt takes the bread and passes it to Rachel. The conversation and laughter start up again. The meal continues. But quietly the bread and wine are circulating, passed from person to person with a word of encouragement or a short prayer. Out into the kitchen where Steve has already started on the washing up. Children are put to bed, the meal is cleared, coffee is made, and pudding is served (always a treat) before we turn to God's Word.

What's so remarkable about this? In one sense, nothing. It's a meal that's repeated thousands of times around the world every day. And yet everything that matters is summed up in this meal. The Bible story is played out. God's new world is glimpsed. Peter Leithart says: "The Lord's Supper is the world in miniature; it has cosmic significance. Within it we find clues to the meaning of all creation and all history, to the nature of God and the nature of man, to the mystery of the world, which is Christ. . . . Though the table stands at the center its effects stretch out to the four corners of the earth."[1]

If your church stopped celebrating communion, what difference would it make to your life?

Luke 22:7–20

Then came the day of Unleavened Bread, on which the Passover lamb had to be sacrificed. So Jesus sent Peter and John, saying, "Go and prepare the Passover for us, that we may eat it." They said to him, "Where will you have us prepare it?" He said to them, "Behold, when you have entered the city, a man carrying a jar of water will meet you. Follow him into the house that he enters and tell the master of the house, 'The Teacher says to you, Where is the guest room, where I may eat the Passover with my disciples?' And he will show you a large upper room furnished; prepare it there." And they went and found it just as he had told them, and they prepared the Passover.

And when the hour came, he reclined at table, and the apostles with him. And he said to them, "I have earnestly desired to eat this Passover with you before I suffer. For I tell you I will not eat it until it is fulfilled in the kingdom of God." And he took a cup, and when he had given thanks, he said, "Take this, and divide it among yourselves. For I tell you that from now on I will not drink of the fruit of the vine until the kingdom of God comes." And he took bread, and when he had given thanks, he broke it and gave it to them, saying, "This is my body, which is given for you. Do this in remembrance of me." And likewise the cup after they had eaten, saying, "This cup that is poured out for you is the new covenant in my blood."

Five times Luke reminds us that this meal is the Passover (vv. 7, 8, 11, 13, 15). The first Passover meal was eaten the night before the exodus, when God liberated his people from slavery in Egypt (Exodus 12). Each family was told to kill a flawless lamb and daub its blood around their door. Then they roasted the lamb and ate it with unleavened bread. That night the Lord passed over the houses daubed with blood, but he killed the firstborn in every Egyptian home, so that Pharaoh finally allowed the Israelites to go free. The Passover lamb rescued God's people from slavery, and it rescued them from death by dying in their place.

The Last Supper looks back on the first Passover meal, but it also looks forward to the messianic banquet promised in Isaiah 25. Jesus says: "I will not eat it until it is fulfilled in the kingdom of God. . . . I will not drink of the fruit of the vine until the kingdom of God comes" (Luke 22:16, 18). "The Eucharist is our model of the eschatological order, a microcosm of the way things really ought to be."[2] In other words, this shared meal is a foretaste of God's coming new world.

Luke has placed the Lord's Supper in the context of the Bible story, looking back to the Passover and forward to the messianic banquet. To understand the Lord's Supper, we need to sketch a biblical theology of food and meals.

Rebellion Embodied in a Meal

Before the fall, food was the way we expressed our obedience and trust in God. We obeyed God by eating from any tree except the tree of the knowledge of good and evil. Eating continues to express our dependence on God and our submission to his good reign. We gratefully receive food in all its wonderful variety as a gift from God (as we saw in chap. 3).

At the fall, food was the way we expressed our disobedience and mistrust of God. It was an attempt to live life without God (expressed through taking forbidden food). Paul says: "Although they knew God, they did not honor him as God or give thanks to him, but they became futile in their thinking, and their foolish hearts were darkened" (Rom. 1:21). As a result of the fall, we would no longer honor God by living by his word, or express gratitude by receiving the food on which we depend as a gift from him.

We are embodied persons, and so sin affects our bodies. No sooner did Adam and Eve rebel against God than they felt ashamed of their bodies. Sin distorts all of our relationships, including our relationships with food.

103

We Use Food for Control Instead of Looking to God's Greatness

My Mexican friend Alejandro is horrified at the way Americans eat food on the move. We're so busy trying to be in control that many of us treat food as fuel. As a result we strip food of its identity as gift, it's "gift-ness." It becomes mere utility. We disregard its rich variety and amazing tastes. Denying that food is a gift allows us to forget the Giver. The moments God gave us to eat, rest, enjoy, commune, and express gratitude are written out of our schedules so we can get on with achieving our own goals. We're too busy proving ourselves or managing our lives without God to stop and express our dependence.

Food is meant to express our dependence on God, but we use food to express our independence *from* God. For my anorexic friend, food became a way of exercising control. In a scary world full of many things she couldn't control, she could at least control what went in her mouth. But, as she herself put it, this practice quickly escalated and became out of control. Anorexia is for some a way to exercise self-sovereignty instead of trusting the sovereignty of God.

We Use Food for Image Instead of Looking to God's Glory

Food can become a means of salvation and deification now, just as it was in the garden of Eden. Satan tells Eve that she and Adam will become like God if they eat the forbidden fruit. Our concern for self-image is an attempt to be godlike. We want to be worshiped. We are concerned with our glory instead of living for God's glory. We fear the rejection of other people instead of fearing God. We are controlled by the opinion of others instead of recognizing God as the glorious one whose opinion is the one that truly matters. Today we still take the fruit—or deny ourselves the cake—to become godlike, people with bodies others will worship and serve. As the model Kate Moss famously said: "Nothing tastes as good as skinny feels."

The tragic irony is that Adam and Eve were already like God, having been made in his image. But we attempt to remake ourselves through food into a form that others will worship.

We Use Food for Refuge Instead of Looking to God's Goodness

We often use food as an escape instead of finding refuge in God. We self-medicate with food. We become priests bringing offerings of chocolate to ourselves. We find comfort in sugar, salt, and fat instead of the living God. The result is ill health and weight gain. Some people then try to manage this through dieting, bulimia, or anorexia. Life without God is an empty life, and we cannot fill that emptiness with food. We miss the opportunity to turn to God. We want to live by bread alone. We find true refuge in the comfort of God and true satisfaction in the goodness of God.

Neither eating to live (food as fuel) nor living to eat (food as salvation) is right. We're to eat to the glory of God and live to the glory of God. When we remove God from our lives, our relationship with food distorts.

We Use Food for Identity Instead of Looking to God's Grace

For some food is aspirational. We use it to express the image or lifestyle to which we aspire. Organic and whole-food produce—these are the things that prove you're enlightened and politically aware. Or maybe it's steaks and burgers—they make you feel like a true man. Or maybe it's pot roasts and home-baked apple pie like your grandmother made—they make you a traditional, all-American mom. Or maybe it's cordon bleu and haute cuisine—they make you an urban and urbane sophisticate. Others manipulate food to prove themselves through their looks by obsessing about their calorie intake. Others are so busy proving themselves through their work that they have little time for food. We use or misuse food to form our identity instead of finding identity in Christ. We use food to achieve identity instead of receiving it by grace.

Slimming programs can offer a kind of points-based religion. Salvation comes through being accepted by others, and a beautiful body is the means by which we save ourselves. Food is rated, so your progress toward salvation can be scored. Your life is assessed when you stand on the scales. Weight loss equals righteousness; weight gain equals condemnation. You are weighed in the scales and found wanting.

The first thing that happens when Adam and Eve eat the fruit is that they feel shame (Gen. 3:7). Still today our attempts at self-salvation through food lead to shame. They generate body-image problems. My friend Jonny Woodrow says: "Eve was the first woman to know the link between self-indulgent eating and having nothing to wear." Parties can be a great celebration of food and friendship. But for some they're filled with temptations and cause nothing but fear. My anorexic friend would avoid social gatherings with food or arrive after the meal. She was fraught with fear when she faced eating in public. For others it's the companions who bring fear. Will I be accepted? Will I be witty, attractive, or intelligent enough?

Promise Embodied in a Meal

The story of God's redeeming our broken world begins with his promise to Abraham—the promise of a people who know God, living in a land of blessing. Abraham's family becomes the nation of Israel, and the defining moment in Israel's history is its exodus from slavery in Egypt.

It's this event that's embodied in the Passover meal. Each year the nation of Israel would commemorate and reenact God's redemption through a meal. The Passover became the identity-defining practice of Israel. It was their theological education. Each Passover, children were to ask about its significance, and the story would be retold.

Through this meal they understood the nature of their God and their own identity. This is theology served up on the meal table.

Not only were the people of Israel rescued through an event encapsulated in a meal, they were rescued *for* a meal. When Israel reached Mount Sinai, the seventy elders went up the mountain where "they beheld God, and ate and drank" (Ex. 24:11). They ate a meal in the presence of God. The Passover represents redemption embodied *in* a meal *for* a meal with God. The land that God promises his people is "a land flowing with milk and honey" (Ex. 3:8) in which "you shall eat and be full, and you shall bless the LORD your God for the good land he has given you" (Deut. 8:10).

But only the leaders eat with God on the mountain. The people are terrified by God's presence. God is dangerous. This reminds us that the problem of sin and judgment must be addressed before we can eat with God.

Israel represents a fresh start, a new humanity. But they have their own temptation story:

> You shall remember the whole way that the LORD your God has led you these forty years in the wilderness, that he might humble you, testing you to know what was in your heart, whether you would keep his commandments or not. And he humbled you and let you hunger and fed you with manna, which you did not know, nor did your fathers know, that he might make you know that man does not live by bread alone, but man lives by every word that comes from the mouth of the LORD. (Deut. 8:2–3)

Israel learned too late that man does not live by bread—or for bread—alone. They repeatedly grumbled against God, because they feared they wouldn't have enough bread or water or meat (Exodus 16–17; Numbers 11). "They spoke against God, saying, 'Can God spread a table in the wilderness?'" (Ps. 78:19). They didn't live in dependence on God, nor did they trust him to lead them into the land of milk and honey (Numbers 13–14). So the whole generation that came out of Egypt died in the wilderness. Meanwhile God provided manna—a bread from heaven that tastes like honey in anticipation of the blessing of the Promised Land. Their first act when Joshua eventually led a new generation into the land was to feast.

The Sabbath law that Israel received at Sinai built the expression of dependence into the eating experience. The Sabbath day is a day without work, and during the Sabbath year the land was to lie fallow. What if this lost work and lost year meant you didn't produce enough food? Your only guarantee was the faithfulness of God. You could never entirely claim to be providing for yourself because one year in seven you did nothing except trust God. The Sabbath laws made eating an act of faith. Man does not live by bread alone.

Deuteronomy 14:22–29

You shall tithe all the yield of your seed that comes from the field year by year. And before the LORD your God, in the place that he will choose, to make his name dwell there, you shall eat the tithe of your grain, of your wine, and of your oil, and the firstborn of your herd and flock, that you may learn to fear the LORD your God always. And if the way is too long for you, so that you are not able to carry the tithe, when the LORD your God blesses you, because the place is too far from you, which the LORD your God chooses, to set his name there, then you shall turn it into money and bind up the money in your hand and go to the place that the LORD your God chooses and spend the money for whatever you desire—oxen or sheep or wine or strong drink, whatever your appetite craves. And you shall eat there before the LORD your God and rejoice, you and your household. And you shall not neglect the Levite who is within your towns, for he has no portion or inheritance with you.

At the end of every three years you shall bring out all the tithe of your produce in the same year and lay it up within your towns. And the Levite, because he has no portion or inheritance with you, and the sojourner, the fatherless, and the widow, who are within your towns, shall come and eat and be filled, that the LORD your God may bless you in all the work of your hands that you do.

Feasts were an integral part of old covenant faith. Every year God's people were to spend one-tenth of their produce on a feast.

Do the math. This was a big party, and on the menu is "whatever you desire" (v. 26). The key element was that it was eaten "before the LORD your God" (v. 26). It was a meal in the presence of God. This is salvation. Every third year the meal was to be eaten locally ("within your towns"), and the immigrants, the poor, the vulnerable were to be invited. The people of God are to be a community in which everyone, however marginal, joins the party.

First Kings 4 describes the high point of Israel's story, during the reign of Solomon. The promise of a people as numerous as the sand on the seashore is fulfilled (v. 20). The promise of a land at peace on all sides is fulfilled, with every man under his own fig tree, enjoying security and provision (vv. 24–25). The promise of blessing to the nations is fulfilled with the kings of the earth sending delegations to learn wisdom from Solomon (vv. 29–34). Central to this fulfillment is food. Solomon's daily provisions are listed in splendid detail (vv. 7–19, 22–28). But it's not just the king who eats well: "Judah and Israel were as many as the sand by the sea. They ate and drank and were happy" (v. 20).

But from here, it's downhill. Solomon marries foreign wives, who lead him into the worship of foreign gods. This sets a pattern for future kings. The kingdom is divided, with the northern kingdom eventually going into exile in Assyria. The southern kingdom, ruled by the Davidic line of kings, limps on until eventually it too is exiled, in Babylon.

The prophets warn of this coming judgment, and they often do so in terms of food. Food is so integral to life, that judgment affects diet. The very first declaration of judgment is when God tells the Serpent that he will eat dust (Gen. 3:14). The Israelites are made to drink the golden calf after Moses has ground it up and combined it with water (Ex. 32:20).

The prophets also speak of restoration after judgment. The promises to Abraham and David still stand. Salvation is also described in dietary language. The renewal of the land will mean the renewal of food.

No one integrates food into his message of salvation and judgment like the prophet Joel. In chapter 1 Joel describes an invading army of locusts. It's not clear whether the passage is describing locusts that are like an army or an army that is like locusts. What is clear is the impact on the diet of God's people. Joel calls on "all you drinkers of wine" to wail "because of the sweet wine, for it is cut off from your mouth" (v. 5). The traditional image of shalom or peace in Israel is that of every man under his own fig tree, but now the fig trees are stripped bare (v. 7). The lack of food is complete: "The fields are destroyed, the ground mourns, because the grain is destroyed, the wine dries up, the oil languishes" (v. 10). At least fifteen of the twenty verses in chapter 1 refer to food. Judgment is the absence of food. As a result, "gladness dries up from the children of man" (v. 12). Food equals gladness. Famine equals judgment.

Blessing is not only that God's people can eat bread and wine, but that they can eat and drink with their God. But now the priests must wail "because grain offering and drink offering are withheld from the house of your God" (Joel 1:13); "Is not the food cut off before our eyes, joy and gladness from the house of our God?" (v. 16).

While Joel 1 describes past events, Joel 2 speaks of a coming day, the day of the Lord. Another locust army is coming—one that is inescapable, invincible, and without precedent: "their like has never been before, nor will be again after them through the years of all generations" (Joel 2:2). In the history of Israel God used invading armies (whether of soldiers or locusts) to judge his people. But a day is coming when God himself will come in judgment against humanity. "The land is like the garden of Eden before them, but behind them a desolate wilderness, and nothing escapes them" (v. 3). God's judgment undoes Eden. It turns the provision and plenty of the garden into a wilderness.

In the light of this greater, coming judgment, the Lord calls on his people to repent or "return" (Joel 2:12–13). This repentance is defined in food-related terms: instead of feasting there is to be fasting (2:15; 1:14).

Hope is found in the character of God, and specifically in the name he revealed to Moses after the Israelites feasted before the golden calf, the archetypal sin of Israel (Ex. 32:5–6; 34:5–7): "Return to the LORD your God, for he is gracious and merciful, slow to anger, and abounding in steadfast love; and he relents over disaster" (Joel 2:13).

If the foundation of hope is God's mercy, the content of hope is eating with God. Joel 2:14 says: "Who knows whether he will not turn and relent, and leave a blessing behind him, a grain offering and a drink offering for the LORD your God?" In Joel 2:3 God left behind wilderness, but in 2:14 he leaves behind grain and wine so God's people can again present their offerings and enjoy community with God. This hope is elaborated in Joel 2:14–27; it's all about eating and the removal of shame:

> The LORD answered and said to his people,
> "Behold, I am sending to you
>> grain, wine, and oil,
>> and you will be satisfied;
> and I will no more make you
>> a reproach among the nations. . . .
> the tree bears its fruit;
>> the fig tree and vine give their full yield. . . .
> The threshing floors shall be full of grain;
>> the vats shall overflow with wine and oil.
> You shall eat in plenty and be satisfied,
>> and praise the name of the LORD your God,
>> who has dealt wondrously with you." (Joel 2:19, 22, 24, 26;
>>> see Jer. 31:11–14)

God's grace is expressed as an abundance of food. Salvation is a feast.

Joel 3 describes how "in those days" God will gather the nations to the valley of judgment. While God's people beat their swords into ploughshares and their spears into pruning hooks, ready to produce a harvest of food (Isa. 2:4), the nations must do the reverse, beating their ploughshares into swords and their pruning hooks into spears, as they prepare to face God's warriors (Joel 3:10). While salvation for God's people means an abundant harvest (2:19), the nations themselves become a harvest of judgment (Joel 2:13; Rev. 14:14–20). "But the LORD is a refuge to his people, a stronghold to the people of Israel" (3:16). He's the gracious King who comes to destroy, but provides a refuge from his own advance through the death of Jesus on our behalf (Ps. 2:12). "And in that day the mountains shall drip sweet wine, and the hills shall flow with milk, and all the streambeds of Judah shall flow with water . . ." (Joel 3:18). This is salvation: to feast abundantly and to feast with God.

Redemption Embodied in a Meal

At the heart of the Bible story, at its turning point, is another meal: the Last Supper. The Last Supper, which becomes for us the Lord's Supper, is a celebration of the story's central act: the cross of Jesus. The Last Supper was not only looking back to the Passover and forward to the messianic banquet, it was also looking ahead to the following day, to the cross:

> He took bread, and when he had given thanks, he broke it and gave it to them, saying, "This is my body, which is given for you. Do this in remembrance of me." And likewise the cup after they had eaten, saying, "This cup that is poured out for you is the new covenant in my blood." (Luke 22:19–20)

Think about the events of that following day. Jesus dies in darkness. Darkness was a sign of God's judgment. Jesus is judged in our place so we can be acquitted. So as he dies, the curtain of the temple is torn in two. This curtain was as thick as a man's hand. It separated people from the Most Holy Place, the heart of the temple and the symbol of God's presence. The curtain separated God from humanity, because his holiness might destroy us in our sin. But at Jesus's death on the cross, sin and judgment are dealt with, and so the curtain is torn in two. The way to God is open. We are invited to celebrate the feast.

Jesus is the host of the messianic banquet, and the Last Supper mirrors this: Peter and John are told to prepare the meal, but the preparations have already been made by Jesus (Luke 22:8–13). On the night before he dies, Jesus tells his disciples that he's going to prepare a place for them in his Father's house (John 14:3–4). Jesus is the host, and he prepares a place for us through the cross. Jesus is the Passover Lamb. His blood is daubed over our lives; the Lord passes over us, and we're redeemed from our empty way of life (1 Pet. 1:18–19). We're redeemed so we can come to the mountain of God, and eat and drink with God.

Jesus's death and resurrection inaugurate a new covenant and a new people. In Luke 4 Jesus recapitulates the temptation story. Luke has just traced the family line of Jesus back to Adam, describing Jesus as "the son of Adam" (3:38). How will this new Adam relate to God through food? Jesus is also the true Israelite; how will this new Israel relate to God through food? Satan's first temptation of Jesus is an invitation to turn stones into bread. Jesus has been fasting for forty days and, just in case we're not sure what this means, Luke tells us "he was hungry" (4:2). Nevertheless Jesus answered, "It is written, 'Man shall not live by bread alone'" (4:4). Jesus is the new humanity and the new Israel, relating to God in trust and obedience.

Just as Israel was constituted by the old Mosaic covenant, the new community of Jesus is founded with a new covenant. "This cup that is poured out for you is the new covenant in my blood" (Luke 22:20). The word "covenant" is a relational term. It signifies a bond of loyalty and commitment. It's a formally agreed-upon promise. At Sinai God promised to be Israel's God if Israel would be his people, but Israel broke the covenant (Jer. 31:31–32). In the new covenant Jesus represents both God and humanity. He is God's Son and the faithful representative of God's people. Therefore this covenant is eternal and secure, because it rests on Christ's perfect faithfulness. He doesn't succumb to temptation. He doesn't live by bread alone. The new covenant promises not only a people who know God, but a people who are renewed. "This is the covenant that I will make with the house of Israel after those days, declares the LORD: I will put my law within them, and I will write it on their hearts. And I will be their God, and they shall be my people. . . . For I will forgive their iniquity, and I will remember their sin no more" (Jer. 31:33–34; see Hebrews 8). God contracts himself to be our Savior, and the contract is signed, sealed, and delivered through the blood of his Son.

Food can be a curse as well as a blessing. We see it in the Bible, and we see it in our world today in excessive dieting, eating disorders, global poverty, and unjust trade. But the gospel offers a better story, which realigns eating. Food is not the source of life. We do not live by bread alone. But food is not forgotten or rendered insignificant. We live "by every word that comes from the mouth of the LORD" (Deut. 8:3). But this word is embodied in a meal. The communion meal reorients life by relocating us in the story told by the Word. Instead of being defined by the stories of our culture, we live as participants in God's story. And the meal points to the goal: eating in the presence of God as a celebration of his generosity in creation and salvation. We anticipate this in every meal, but especially in the Lord's Supper.

Hope Embodied in a Meal

On the day of Pentecost Peter quotes from Joel 2:28–32 (Acts 2:14–21). The feast promised by Joel has begun. We know from the parables of

114

the kingdom in Matthew 13 and Mark 4 that while the kingdom of God will one day come in glory and judgment, it first comes in a secret way through the gracious invitation of the gospel message. As Joel describes the last days, he twice says the sun will be turned to darkness (2:31; 3:15). Peter's use of Joel 2:31 on the day of Pentecost suggests that this was fulfilled as the Son of Man died in darkness on the cross to redeem his people and rose again to ascend on the clouds in glory to the presence of God. From there he has poured out his Spirit on his people. The climactic conflict involving all humanity described in Joel 3 is still to come. But the feast of the new age has begun with the presence of the Spirit. The mountains don't yet drip new wine, nor do the hills flow with milk (3:18). Life in the not-yet-renewed earth can often be hard. But there's a real sense in which the feast that the prophets promised has begun.

This feast is not simply a metaphor. That would be Gnosticism, the movement that plagued the early church with its message of escape from the physical world through enlightenment. Peter Leithart argues that the bread we eat in communion tells us that the future new creation is not a "cancellation of this-worldly concerns."[3] Rather, it's this world transformed. Eating communion bread is the beginning and sign of the new creation. And the fact that it's prepared bread, not plain wheat, suggests the cultural, social, and technological structures required for its production will also be renewed.

When the disparate people of God come together and express community around the table, united as we are in Christ, then the promised feast finds fulfillment. When we celebrate the goodness of creation as we enjoy our food, then the promised feast finds fulfillment, and we anticipate the renewal of creation. When we eat together in the presence of God by his Spirit, then the promised feast finds fulfillment. These are powerful declarations to the world of the coming feast of God to which all humanity is invited and the current presence of God with his people. Joel himself declares at the climax of his prophecy: "the LORD dwells in Zion" (3:21).

I think of my own missional community. A dozen or so people of all ages and backgrounds eat together on a Thursday night around the table: enjoying simple food yet relishing it (as we do) as a good gift from God; celebrating together what the Spirit has been doing in our lives; praying for the needs of the world; and discussing how we can bless our neighborhood in Christ's name. This is a fulfillment of the feast promised by Isaiah and Joel. And this is an anticipation of the eternal banquet. When we share bread and wine, presenting our grain and drink offerings to God (not as an atonement for sin, but as a thanksgiving for Christ's once-for-all atonement), then the promised feast finds fulfillment.

Eating between the Beginning and Final Fulfillment of the Feast

Jesus said, "I have earnestly desired to eat this Passover with you before I suffer. For I tell you I will not eat it until it is fulfilled in the kingdom of God" (Luke 22:15–16). Before Jesus comes into his kingdom, he must first suffer. The good news that Jesus proclaimed was the coming of God's kingdom. This is good news, because God's kingdom is a rule of justice, peace, joy, freedom, and life. Satan's lie in the garden portrayed God's rule as bad news, and ever since then, we've thought we'll be more free without God—only to end up enslaved. So God's coming kingdom is good news. But we're all rebels against God's rule, and for rebels God's coming rule means judgment. For us, God's coming kingdom is bad news. But here's the wonderful twist in the story: When the King comes to his world, judgment falls not on rebellious humanity, but on the King himself at the cross. Jesus bore the judgment we deserve, so that repentant rebels can experience the coming of his kingdom as good news.

We find in Jesus a pattern of suffering followed by glory. Followers of Jesus must follow the same pattern. Our sufferings aren't redemptive, but we are called to follow Christ's example of sacrificial love and service. Jesus said, "If anyone would come after me, let him deny himself and take up his cross daily and follow me" (9:23). Paul said we're "heirs with Christ, provided we suffer with him in order that we may also be glorified with him" (Rom. 8:17). He strengthens and encourages new churches by telling them that "through many tribulations we must enter the kingdom of God" (Acts 14:22).

But the disciples don't get it. At the Last Supper they begin arguing about who's the greatest.

Luke 22:24–30

A dispute also arose among them, as to which of them was to be regarded as the greatest. And he said to them, "The kings of the Gentiles exercise lordship over them, and those in authority over them are called benefactors. But not so with you. Rather, let the greatest among you become as the youngest, and the leader as one who serves. For who is the greater, one who reclines at table or one who serves? Is it not the one who reclines at table? But I am among you as the one who serves.

"You are those who have stayed with me in my trials, and I assign to you, as my Father assigned to me, a kingdom, that you may eat and drink at my table in my kingdom and sit on thrones judging the twelve tribes of Israel."

The disciples were probably angling for positions of honor around the table like the Pharisees in Luke 14. They want honor without service. They want glory without suffering. Jesus calls them to the way of the cross, the way of humility and love. Jesus goes on to give this remarkable promise: if you endure suffering with me, then you will experience the glory of my eternal feast. They want glory without suffering. Jesus promises suffering followed by glory. If you follow the way of the cross, then you will experience the glory of the resurrection.

Jesus says, "I have earnestly desired to eat this Passover with you before I suffer. For I tell you I will not eat it until it is fulfilled in the kingdom of God" (Luke 22:15–16). He longs to eat it. He longs for a meal with friends. Why? Because this meal with friends is a foretaste of his kingdom. This is why he must suffer: so that his people can come to the mountain and eat with God. Jesus will experience in the Supper a glimpse of the goal of his work of salvation. In that experience he will be reassured that the suffering that weighs so heavy on his heart is worth it. This is what it is for: sharing community around a meal table with his people.

The meal functions in the same way for us. What we call "the Lord's Supper" is a foretaste of "the Lamb's Supper" in Revelation 19. It's a beginning of the feast we eat with Jesus and his people in the new creation. It's not just a picture. It's the real thing begun in a partial way. We eat with God's people, and we eat with the ascended Christ, present through the Holy Spirit.

The Lord's Supper should be a meal we "earnestly desire" to eat. We should approach it with anticipation. With longing. With excitement. With joy. The Lord's Supper should be a joyous occasion. A vibrant meal with friends. A feast.

Our earnest desire must surely affect how we celebrate the Lord's Supper. Today it has commonly become ritualized. We're the group in town whose central meal involves a fragment of bread and a small sip of wine. How is this a foretaste of the messianic banquet?

The bread and wine in the New Testament are part of a meal. Luke says of the Jerusalem church, "Breaking bread in their homes, they received their food with glad and generous hearts" (Acts 2:46). Commentators often can't decide whether this refers to meals in general or Communion. That's because we assume they're two different things. We think of a meal taking place around the dining table at home while we think of Communion as a solemn rite in a church building. But in Jerusalem followers of Jesus ate meals together in their homes, eating bread, drinking wine, remembering Jesus, and celebrating the community he created through his death.

These were feasts of friends. Some in the church at Corinth were abusing the meals, but Paul doesn't tell them to separate the bread and wine from the meal. Quite the opposite. He tells them to wait for one another so they can eat the meal together. Communion should be a feast of friends shared with laughter, tears, prayers, and stories. We celebrate the community life that God gives us through the cross and in the Spirit. We can't celebrate it with heads bowed and eyes closed, alone in our private thoughts and strangely solitary even as we're surrounded by other people.

When we recapture the Lord's Supper as a feast of friends, celebrated as a meal in the presence of the Spirit, then it will become something we earnestly desire. It will become the high point of our life together as the people of God. In this sad and broken world, the Lord's Supper is a moment of joy, because it's a moment of the future.

Why a Meal?

Why bread and wine? Why didn't Jesus say, "Say this in remembrance of me"? Why give us physical substances to eat and drink? I sometimes wonder whether some evangelicals would prefer it if we did indeed drop the bread and wine and replace them with a form of words.

Most Communion debates focus on the status of the bread and wine. But the bread and wine are part of a wider social event with a community, a liturgy (however informal), prayers, and Bible readings. The bread doesn't mystically change us, as if it were some kind of magic potion. But neither is it merely a memory aid that touches our minds alone. It's part of a wider shared experience. "The character of the kingdom is revealed not in a substantial transformation of the bread and wine, or in the absence of such a transformation, or in a believer's individual communion, but in the whole action of the common meals."[4] Sharing a meal with other people in the presence of the Holy Spirit, breaking a loaf that someone has baked, remembering together the cross, praying together—all these things affect us. The Lord's Supper is more than a mere memorial. It changes us. "Because there is one bread, we who are many are one body, for we all partake of the one bread" (1 Cor. 10:17). The shared activity of partaking of the one loaf forms us afresh as one body. It reinforces our identity as a community shaped by the cross.

Paul expresses a similar idea when discussing food offered to idols in 1 Corinthians 8–10, an argument that ends at the Communion table. Meat on its own—even meat offered to idols—has no significance other than being food from God (1 Cor. 8:4–8). The blessing of a pagan priest doesn't transform it. So Paul feels free to eat meat previously offered to idols. But put the food and the idols together in the relational context of a pagan ceremony, and everything changes. It's the social context that gives the food meaning—so much so that participation in the event is a participation with demons. "What do I imply then? That food offered to idols is anything, or that an idol is anything? No, I imply that what pagans sacrifice they offer to demons and not to God. I do not want you to be participants with demons" (1 Cor. 10:19–20).

In the same way, the bread and wine on their own have no special meaning, and the blessing of a priest doesn't transform them. It's the social context that gives them meaning—so much so that participation in the event is a participation in the body and blood of Christ: "The cup of blessing that we bless, is it not a participation in the blood of Christ? The bread that we break, is it not a participation in the body of Christ?" (10:16).

So why a meal with bread and wine?

The Meal Is an Act of Remembrance

"This is my body, which is given for you. Do this in remembrance of me" (Luke 22:19).

The Gettysburg Address is routinely reenacted in schools across the United States. The cotton wool industry is kept afloat by seven-year-olds wearing fake Abraham Lincoln beards. What's the effect of this practice? It has shaped generation after generation of young Americans. It gives a sense of national identity and reinforces values of freedom and democracy. It matters, too, that this speech is not merely learned at home, but is publicly enacted. Those in the room are bound together by what happens on the stage. This is how Passover worked for Israelites, and this is how the Lord's Supper works in the church.

The Lord's Supper may be more than a memorial, but it's certainly not less than a memorial. Each time we participate, we're reminded of the cross. We're reminded that our sin is atoned for. We're free, forgiven, acquitted, adopted. And we're reminded that the cross is our model. We're called afresh to serve and to sacrifice.

Communion is a reminder to us. But it may also be a reminder to God. The words we so often hear, "do this in remembrance of me," are literally "do this for my memorial" (see Lev. 2:2, 9, 16; 5:12). Just as the rainbow in the covenant with Noah was given not to remind us of God's love, but to remind God of his promises (Gen. 9:12–17), so perhaps the bread and wine are to remind God of his new covenant. When God remembers his covenant, it doesn't mean he's previously forgotten, but that he's about to act in keeping with his covenant (Ex. 6:5–6). The Lord's Supper is a call to God to act in keeping with his covenant: forgiving us, accepting us, and welcoming us to the Table through the finished work of Christ.

The Meal Is an Act of Community

"Because there is one bread, we who are many are one body, for we all partake of the one bread" (1 Cor. 10:17).

The Lord's Supper declares the death of Jesus not just in the symbolism of bread and wine, but in the community created by the cross. We've seen time and again how meals create and reinforce community. Christ told us to take bread and wine because they form a meal that binds us together as a community.

This is why what's happening in Corinth so offends Paul. The church's Communion meal reveals its divisions. Indeed, division seems to have been the goal for some. In the culture of the day it was common for banquets to be "occasions for the conspicuous display of social distance and even for humiliation of the clients of the rich, by means of the quality and quantity of food provided to different tables."[5] The wealthy in Corinth were using the Lord's Supper in this way to highlight their social superiority. But, says Paul, this is not the purpose of the Lord's Supper. That kind of meal doesn't proclaim the Lord's death. We proclaim his death by eating together as a reconciled community through the cross. The cross humbles us all as we see the extent of sin, and the cross exalts us all as we're welcomed into God's family. The family that eats together stays together.

The Meal Is an Act of Dependence

"Man shall not live by bread alone" (Luke 4:4).

Every meal is a reminder of our dependence, as creatures, on God—the Communion meal included. Each mouthful is a reminder that we're not self-sustaining. We may not live by bread alone, but we do live by bread. We must pray: "Give us each day our daily bread" (Luke 11:3).

But the Communion meal is also a recognition of our dependence on God as sinners. We live by the death of his Son. "Man does not live by bread alone, but man lives by every word that comes from the mouth of the LORD" (Deut. 8:3). We live by the word of the cross. Each mouthful is a reminder that we cannot save ourselves. We eat bread, rather than merely say some words, to remind us that we rely on his grace afresh each day just as much as we rely on our daily bread.

The Meal Is an Act of Participation

"The cup of blessing that we bless, is it not a participation in the blood of Christ? The bread that we break, is it not a participation in the body of Christ?" (1 Cor. 10:16).

We're not observers around the Communion table. We're participants. We do something. We ingest something. If the Eucharist involved just some words, then we'd be mere hearers, passively observing the drama of salvation at a distance. But bread and wine draw us in. This salvation becomes our salvation. Objectively our salvation doesn't depend on participation in the Lord's Supper. It's not a magic meal. But the Lord's Supper is described as "communion" or "participation." Through the Communion meal, salvation becomes a subjective reality for us afresh. We enact our union with Christ, and in him find we're forgiven, justified, and adopted.

The Meal Is an Act of Formation

"For as often as you eat this bread and drink the cup, you proclaim the Lord's death until he comes" (1 Cor. 11:26).

On January 15, 2009, US Airways flight 1549 departing from LaGuardia Airport, New York, ran into a flock of geese shortly after takeoff, and both engines lost power. There was every chance the plane would crash, with the loss of all on board and many hundreds more in the city below. But amazingly Captain Chesley Sullenberger managed to land the plane on the Hudson River, and no one was killed. Sullenberger had no time to consult a manual or discuss his options in detail. What enabled him to pull off his dramatic landing was years of experience. In the moment of crisis the habits learned over the years kicked in, and the pilot brought everyone down safely.

Participation in the Communion meal is habit-forming. The Lord's Supper is a drama in which we're active participants. Each time we participate, we're learning and relearning our role. We're learning the habits of cross-centered living. Leithart describes the Supper as "the church's role-play":

> Though the Eucharist does not bypass the mind and conscious reflection, the effect it has is more in the realm of acquiring a skill than in the realm of learning a new set of facts; the effect is more a matter of "training" than "teaching." At the Supper, we eat bread and

123

drink wine together with thanksgiving not merely to *show* the way things really ought to be but to *practice* the way things really ought to be. . . . Not automatically, but in the context of biblical teaching and a robust community life, the skills and virtues practiced at the Lord's table will spill over to fill the whole church with a Eucharistic ethos. In short, the Supper exercises the church in the protocols of life in the presence of God.[6]

In a busy culture with people desperate to succeed, we practice in Communion resting on the finished work of Christ. In a fragmented culture that is radically individualistic, we practice in Communion belonging to one another. In a dissatisfied culture of constant striving, we practice in Communion receiving this world with joy as a gift from God. In a narcissistic culture of self-fulfillment, we practice in Communion joyous self-denial and service. In a proud culture of self-promotion, we practice in Communion humility and generosity. All these practices are habit-forming, and so seep into the rest of our lives.

After all this has been said, remember Jesus didn't say, "Think this in remembrance of me." The Lord's Supper serves its purposes not when it's written about in books, but when it's shared in the Christian community.

6

Meals as Enacted Promise

Luke 24

"They gave him a piece of broiled fish, and he took it and ate before them." (Luke 24:42–43)

The risen Christ eats. The Son of Man came eating and drinking. And still the Son of Man eats. The physicality of Jesus is not cancelled by the resurrection. His humanity doesn't morph into some ethereal existence. In the heretical Gnostic Gospels, written in the centuries after the resurrection, the risen Christ is a ghostly figure. But in the true Gospels, he can be touched. He can eat. And he does so publicly. He "ate before them." He wants to be seen eating so that we will realize that resurrection is not the negation of creation, but its renewal and fulfillment. The resurrection of Jesus is the promise and beginning of the renewal of all things, and the future is a physical future on a renewed earth. It's a future with broiled fish. We will enjoy not just food, but cooking and fermenting and brewing. "On this mountain the LORD of hosts will make for all peoples a feast of rich food, a feast of well-aged wine, of rich food full of marrow, of aged wine well refined" (Isa. 25:6).

In Genesis 3 sin instantly affected physical bodies. As soon as the first man and woman eat the forbidden fruit, they feel shame: "Then the eyes of both were opened, and they knew that they were naked. And they sewed fig leaves together and made themselves loincloths" (Gen. 3:7). Soon it would be felt in the pains of childbirth and the sweat of toil (vv. 16–19). Ultimately it would be felt in death and the return to dust (v. 19).

But salvation, too, is experienced in the body. Jesus is the firstborn from the among the dead, the firstfruits of a great harvest. And he is embodied. He eats (Luke 24:42–43). He cooks (John 21:9–14). He says: "Come and have breakfast" (John 21:12).

Luke 24:13–35

That very day two of them were going to a village named Emmaus, about seven miles from Jerusalem, and they were talking with each other about all these things that had happened. While they were talking and discussing together, Jesus himself drew near and went with them. But their eyes were kept from recognizing him. And he said to them, "What is this conversation that you are holding with each other as you walk?" And they stood still, looking sad. Then one of them, named Cleopas, answered him, "Are you the only visitor to Jerusalem who does not know the things that have happened there in these days?" And he said to them, "What things?" And they said to him, "Concerning Jesus of Nazareth, a man who was a prophet mighty in deed and word before God and all the people, and how our chief priests and rulers delivered him up to be condemned to death, and crucified him. But we had hoped that he was the one to redeem Israel. Yes, and besides all this, it is now the third day since these things happened. Moreover, some women of our company amazed us. They were at the tomb early in the morning, and when they did not find his body, they came back saying that they had even seen a vision of angels, who said that he was alive. Some of those who were with us went to the tomb and found it just as the women had said, but him they did not see." And he said to them, "O foolish ones, and slow of heart to believe all that the prophets have spoken! Was it not necessary that the Christ should suffer these things and enter into his glory?" And beginning with Moses and all the Prophets, he interpreted to them in all the Scriptures the things concerning himself.

So they drew near to the village to which they were going. He acted as if he were going farther, but they urged him strongly, saying, "Stay with us, for it is toward evening and the day is now far spent." So he went in to stay with them. When he was at table with them, he took the bread and blessed and broke it and gave it to them. And their eyes were opened, and they recognized him. And he vanished from their sight. They said to each other, "Did not our hearts burn within us while he talked to us on the road, while he opened to us the Scriptures?" And they rose that same hour and returned to Jerusalem. And they found the eleven and those who were with them gathered together, saying, "The Lord has risen indeed, and has appeared to Simon!" Then they told what had happened on the road, and how he was known to them in the breaking of the bread.

We Live between Good Friday and Easter Sunday

One of our problems is that we know the end of the Emmaus story so well. We know that Jesus is risen. So we find it hard to enter into the disappointment and grief of these disciples. "We had hoped," they say (Luke 24:21).

Yet many people today are following their own version of the Emmaus road. They're walking away from hope. They're walking in disappointment. For many this involves walking away from the church.

Christ doesn't begin with a resurrection pronouncement. He begins with a question: "What is this conversation that you are holding with each other as you walk? . . ." (Luke 24:17). He gives them space to tell their story, to share their pain, to speak their disappointment. Luke captures the drama of it: "And they stood still, looking sad" (v. 17). They're walking, but they have to stop before they can begin.

We need to begin our interaction with people with a question much more often than we do. Only as we enter into their stories, their hopes, and their disappointments will our message connect and have meaning. We mustn't fear others' pain or hide our own, for Christ is with us even if we don't always recognize him.

We need to be willing to engage in an act of imagination that places us alongside these broken people as they retreat to the countryside,

127

escaping from the scene of the holocaust that has shattered their faith in God and his Messiah and left them facing a future without horizons. When we begin at this point, then this familiar narrative starts to resonate afresh in our contemporary historical and cultural situation. Millions of people in our world at the start of the third millennium find themselves walking a pathway that brings them very close to the lonely two on the road to Emmaus. . . . Christian mission, and in particular the practice of evangelism, has often ignored the order I am suggesting here, wanting to reverse the sequence in this story by beginning at the end, declaring the triumph of the resurrection without listening to the indications of pain, doubt and anger of those who have turned away from Jerusalem. The result is that the message declared by Christians is simply unbelievable for people whose emotional and spiritual experience renders them incapable of receiving such a message while their gapping wounds still require healing.[1]

It's not just individuals who are walking their own version of the Emmaus road. Our whole world is between Good Friday and Easter Sunday. "We had hoped," our culture says. Modernity was full of hope, full of visions of progress. Capitalism. Socialism. Scientific progress. Liberalism. All were driven by derivative forms of Christian hope. All shared a sense that history was an onward march. But postmodernity recognizes the dark side of progress. The endemic poverty. The pollution of the planet. The social fragmentation. It distrusts the grand narratives of progress. "We had hoped."

We live in a world in which the biblical story seems out of place. Christianity seems passé and anachronistic. We live in a world in which, functionally, God is dead. That was the cry of the German philosopher Friedrich Nietzsche. Nietzsche claimed not only that "God is dead," but that it's we who've killed him. For Nietzsche this "truth" represents the triumph of human freedom. We no longer need God to make our way in the world. We can live without him. So public discourse takes place without God. Our culture is on the Emmaus road, heading away from Jerusalem.

In 1618 the Spanish artist Diego Velázquez depicted the Emmaus meal in a painting called *Kitchen Maid with the Supper of Emmaus*. Jesus and the disciples are portrayed in the top left corner. But the picture focuses all our attention on the maid. The astonished look on her face as she overhears their conversation suggests she's realized that a previously dead man has just eaten her food. The meal is hinted at, but it's all washed and tidied away. The central item is a piece of rag. The new world has collided with the old.

Sometime after it was finished, the painting was altered by its new owner. The Emmaus scene was covered over entirely, and a few inches were cut from the left-hand margin (so that even in the restored version one of the disciples is missing). The original version was only rediscovered in 1933, when the painting was cleaned.[2] In the altered painting, the resurrected Christ had been edited out of the picture. The Bible story was painted over. Our culture has removed the transcendent, the divine, the eschatological. What we're left with is the washing up. We're left with rags.

Yet this is where we belong. At the sink with rags. In a broken world. Christ's resurrection is the promise of a new world. But we have not yet received resurrection bodies and our world has not yet been renewed (Rom. 8:22–25). It remains under the sign of the cross. We live in a godless and godforsaken world—a world still under God's curse. As Christians we have resurrection life, but we have it so we might live the way of the cross. We live between the cross and resurrection, between Good Friday and Easter Sunday.

For now Christ is incognito. He is what the Reformers, following Paul, called "the hidden Christ." Paul says: "For you have died, and your life is hidden with Christ in God. When Christ who is your life appears, then you also will appear with him in glory" (Col. 3:3–4). The return of Christ is more often described in the New Testament as a manifestation. The reign of Christ is now hidden. But one day it will be manifest. All the earth will see his glory and every knee will bow.

For now, though, we live as disciples of the cross. We embrace obscurity, hiddenness, weakness, marginality, and smallness. The kitchen maid in Velázquez's painting appears to be an African slave. The artist lived in a time when Spain was debating the status of slaves, and Velázquez emphasizes the maid's dignity by portraying her as listening intently to Christ's words. She may be unnoticed by the world around her, but she dominates the painting and therefore our attention. The last shall be first. This is God's way. His kingdom grows unnoticed by the world. It's yeast in dough. It's seed that grows unseen. It's through the cross that Christ reigns in the world.

So we walk alongside people on the Emmaus road not as victors, nor as people with all the answers, but as fellow human beings, fellow sinners, and fellow strugglers. Otherwise the rumor of resurrection will always sound incredible or glib.

In Luke 24:18 the disciples imply that Jesus is ignorant. But when Jesus opens the Bible for them, he begins: "O foolish ones, and slow of heart to believe all that the prophets have spoken! . . ." (v. 25). They had read the Bible, but they'd misread it. Their description of Jesus as "a prophet mighty in deed and word before God and all the people" (v. 19) echoes the epitaph of Moses in Deuteronomy 34:10–12, which suggests they had hoped Jesus was a new Moses bringing a new exodus from Roman rule. "We had hoped that he was the one to redeem Israel . . ." (Luke 24:21). Jesus's followers had domesticated God, making him just the God of Israel. They'd looked for glory and missed the note of suffering. They'd wanted God's blessings, but not God himself. They'd wanted God's blessings, but had not reckoned with their sin. We, too, can look for success without suffering, for blessing without God, for glory that ignores atonement.

We live at a unique time in history. Christianity no longer dominates our culture. We live after Christendom in an increasingly secular culture. The Bible story seems out of place and archaic. People have removed Christ from their worldview, just as someone did to Velázquez's painting.

But don't despair. This is a moment of opportunity to rediscover authentic apostolic Christianity shaped by the cross. The glory, power, and wisdom of Christ, says Paul in 1 Corinthians 1, are seen in the shame, weakness, and foolishness of the cross. And they're seen in the cross-centered lives of those who follow Christ. Our resurrection life is revealed in our conformity to Christ in his death (2 Cor. 4:10–12). We make God known to a post-Christian world by revealing him in cross-centered discipleship.[3]

Christ Is Known through His Word

In a world in which Christ is incognito, how is he known? The Emmaus story provides two interweaving answers. First, Christ is known through his word.

In Acts 1:3 Luke says Jesus appeared to his disciples over a forty-day period. Yet in Luke's Gospel we get three stories that all take place in one day: early morning at the tomb, afternoon on the Emmaus road, and evening in Jerusalem. And all three stories follow the same pattern:

- People are bewildered, disappointed, and fearful (Luke 24:4–5, 18, 21–22, 37).
- They are rebuked (Luke 24:5–6, 25, 38–39).
- They are taught Christ's words or the Scriptures (Luke 24:6–8, 27, 44–45).
- They are told that the message of God's Word is that the Christ must suffer and die (Luke 24:7, 26, 46).
- The result is that they go and tell others (Luke 24:9, 33–34, 47–48).

The implication is that the disciples shouldn't have been bewildered, because they should have realized from the words of Jesus and the Scriptures that the Christ had to suffer and die. The sign of the resurrection at work in people's lives is this: they understand what the Bible teaches about the cross and want to tell others.

Here in Luke 24 is the Word incarnate, freshly risen from the grave. Surely he will simply speak, and the world will listen. But instead he chooses to conduct a Bible study. If the risen Christ on that first Easter day made himself known through the word, then we shouldn't suppose we can make him known in any other way. No amount of human wisdom or philosophy or contemplation apart from the Bible will tell you the meaning of Jesus's resurrection. No one in the Easter story has a clue what's going on until Jesus explains it from the Bible. Only the exposition of the word will make people's hearts burn (v. 32).

What was the message of that first Easter day? Not just the resurrection, but the cross. The point is this: the Easter message is not only that someone has risen. We had already seen that happen in the rising of Lazarus. The Easter message is that *the Crucified One* is risen. "He showed them his hands and his feet" (v. 40). The One who was made sin has risen. The One who died our death. The One who stood in our place. The One who was forsaken by God. The One who was rejected by the world. This is the One who has risen!

"We had hoped that he was the one to redeem Israel," say the disciples (v. 21). The implication is clear. Hope is gone because Jesus has died, and a dead Messiah cannot bring liberation. But the message of the Scriptures is that the Christ *had* to suffer and die *in order to* redeem. Only a dead Christ can redeem. Only a Christ who dies in our place can redeem us from the penalty of our sin. Christ's followers thought that the cross demonstrated that Jesus couldn't be the Messiah, but the Scriptures show that the cross proves he is the Messiah.

Jesus "was delivered up for our trespasses and raised for our justification" (Rom. 4:25). "Justification" is a legal term, the declaration that someone is in the right. The resurrection is that declaration. It

132

declares that the price is paid. Suppose I commit a crime and am sentenced to five years' imprisonment. I'm not a free man until my sentence is served. But after five years, the warden will call me into his office and tell me that my sentence is complete. As far as the judicial system is concerned, there's no further penalty to pay. I'm a free man. The resurrection was the declaration that the penalty for sin is paid. At the resurrection Jesus walked free from the sentence of death. The sentence had been paid in full. And we walked free with him.

Luke calls on Theophilus to believe the promise of a great reversal at the end of history. The ministry of Jesus is the evidence of this future, especially his meals. But the cross and resurrection are the ultimate reversal. The condemned One is vindicated. The dead One is risen. The shamed One is glorified. Here's the great reversal at the end of history already taking place in the middle of history. Here's the sign of what's coming.

In Luke 16 Jesus tells the story of a beggar called Lazarus who lives at the gate of a rich man. Upon dying, Lazarus goes to Abraham's side, while the rich man goes to Hades. The rich man asks Abraham to send Lazarus with water to cool his pain. When the rich man is refused, he makes a second request. He asks for Lazarus to be sent to his brothers to warn of God's judgment. Abraham replies: "If they do not hear Moses and the Prophets, neither will they be convinced if someone should rise from the dead" (16:31). God's Word is enough. Nothing will persuade us if God's Word doesn't persuade us—not even apparitions of the dead. In Luke 24 someone has come back from the dead—just as the rich man requested. But what he does is proclaim the Word of God.

In Emmaus Jesus makes himself known at the moment in the story at which he disappears: "Their eyes were opened, and they recognized him. And he vanished from their sight" (Luke 24:31). Jesus disappears, but his word remains. This is Luke's message to us. How do we make Christ known? Through the Bible. It may not sound trendy, but it's God's way. God rules through his Word, and he extends that rule through his Word.

The same theme is evident in another meal of Jesus.

Luke 10:38–42

Now as they went on their way, Jesus entered a village. And a woman named Martha welcomed him into her house. And she had a sister called Mary, who sat at the Lord's feet and listened to his teaching. But Martha was distracted with much serving. And she went up to him and said, "Lord, do you not care that my sister has left me to serve alone? Tell her then to help me." But the Lord answered her, "Martha, Martha, you are anxious and troubled about many things, but one thing is necessary. Mary has chosen the good portion, which will not be taken away from her."

This is a story of conflict between two sisters. Nothing surprising about that—siblings having been fighting since Cain and Abel. We think we know who's in the right and who's in the wrong. Martha is serving; Mary's doing nothing. Our sympathies are with Martha. She's been left with all the work. The surprising thing is this: Jesus sides with Mary. Martha's question in the original Greek is phrased in a way that shows she expects a positive answer. In English we might phrase it something like: "It's not fair that I have to do all the work, is it?" How could anyone disagree? But Jesus rebukes Martha.

Martha is attending to herself as a hostess rather than attending to Jesus her guest. Luke says, "Martha was distracted with much serving" (Luke 10:40). Distracted from what? The contrast is with Mary, "who sat at the Lord's feet and listened to his teaching" (v. 39). Martha is distracted from Jesus. Some of us have to learn that our guests matter more than our hospitality. Our aim is to serve, not impress.

But it's not simply the presence of Jesus to which Mary pays attention. The challenge of this story is to be attentive to God's Word. Jesus says to Martha: "You are anxious and troubled about many things" (Luke 10:41). The word "anxious" is the same word

134

Luke uses in the story of the sower: "As for what fell among the thorns, they are those who hear, but as they go on their way they are choked by the cares [anxieties] and riches and pleasures of life, and their fruit does not mature" (Luke 8:14). Martha is distracted from hearing the Word of God by anxieties.

Martha is not an enemy of the Word. She's not "ashamed of [Jesus] and of [his] words" (Luke 9:26). Like many people in churches today, she has not rejected Jesus's words. But she's distracted. We're distracted by our careers, homes, holidays, gadgets, image, and investments. Jesus says that one thing is necessary: to sit at his feet and listen to his Word.

This story doesn't promote a spirituality of disengagement or a contemplative life. It offers a word of invitation. It reorients us to the Word that promises a future banquet. This promise liberates us from the worries of this world so that we can put first God's kingdom. Sustained by the words of Jesus, we're set free to care for those we meet on the road whom others pass by, like the Samaritan in the preceding story, despite the risks and the costs (Luke 10:30–35).

Christ Is Known around the Table

> When he was at table with them, he took the bread and blessed and broke it and gave it to them. And their eyes were opened, and they recognized him. . . . Then they told what had happened on the road, and how he was known to them in the breaking of the bread. (Luke 24:30–31, 35)

There are resonances here of the feeding of the five thousand. Both take place as the day is wearing away (Luke 9:12; 24:29). Both are preceded by other suggestions about the identity of Jesus, including that he might be a new Moses. Both involve the same sequence of Jesus taking bread, blessing it, breaking it, and giving it. The meal for the five thousand was the means in Luke's story by which Jesus becomes known as the Messiah. Now the meal at Emmaus is the means by which Jesus becomes known as the suffering Messiah. Jesus is known at the breaking of bread, at the meal table, sharing food with friends and enemies. Christ is known in community.

We're not saying we can separate Christ known around the table from Christ known through his Word. We're not talking about some kind of mystical knowledge, but rather the Word embodied in a meal. The two disciples on the road to Emmaus immediately connect the Word and the meal. Their eyes were opened around the table because the Scriptures were opened to them on the road (Luke 24:31–32). Nevertheless, their testimony is that "he was known to them in the breaking of the bread" (v. 35).

This is my experience: The Christian community often wears me out, winds me up, and drives me crazy. But I also have moments when I look at my brothers and sisters and know the presence of the risen Christ. It's not that my community is anything special. Yet there are moments when I see Christ incognito among the rag-tag people sitting in my front room—and then it seems he's gone again. You see it in our diversity—a diversity that has no explanation except the work of God. You see it when people's hearts burn as God's Word is interpreted. You see it in the love people show to one another.

"We had hoped," the disciples say, "that he was the one to redeem Israel" (Luke 24:21). They had a political hope for power, influence, and glory. But Christ is known at the margins of the world. The resurrection is revealed first to women, whose testimony is treated with suspicion. The future of Christianity lies not in a return to the dominance of Christendom, but in small, intimate communities of light. Often they're unseen by history. But they're what transform neighborhoods and cities.

In my city of Sheffield, winter evenings are dark. As you walk our cold, dark streets, with houses close to the pavement, you can see into people's homes. I often wonder what passers-by make of our church gatherings when they look in. It creates for me a lovely image of mission. We live in a cold and dark world. But when people look in through the window, they see a community of joy, love, and friendship—a place of light and warmth and welcome. This is what the church must be in our dark, cold, loveless world: a place of light *at street level.*

Return to the City

In 1602 Italian artist Caravaggio also painted the meal at Emmaus. His portrayal of Christ is unusual for his time in that Christ is beardless, perhaps representing the disciples' failure initially to recognize him. The picture captures the dramatic moment of recognition. One man is in the act of pushing his chair away in astonishment. But there's also a sense in which he's pushing the chair out toward us. It's as if he's creating space for us to move into the picture. Jesus's arms are extended, notionally in blessing, but in fact inviting us forward. As if that weren't enough, a basket of fruit is teetering on the edge of the table, demanding that we leap into the picture to catch it. Caravaggio is trying to lure us into the scene as active participants.

An encounter with Christ is a call to action, to involvement, to participation. You can't remain a passive observer. For the two disciples, meeting the risen Christ results in a radical change of plan: they literally retrace their steps by returning to the city. Think of how significant that is. They do what they'd urged Christ not to do—they take the road at night with all its attendant dangers (Luke 24:29). But more than that, in the morning they had been followers of an executed traitor, fleeing arrest. In the evening they return to the city. They return to a mission filled with threats and dangers (22:35–38), one that will take them to all nations (Luke 24:47). But they return, because now everything has changed.

There's an important sense in which the messages of secularism and the cross are the same: God is dead, and the world is without God. The difference is that this is where the message of secularism ends, but it's where the message of the cross begins. The scientific

137

revolution, the Enlightenment, and modernity all lead to this terrible conclusion: God is dead, and we live in the world without him.

But this is where the message of the cross begins. God has died, and the world was without God. But on the third day he rose again. Forsaken by God, Christ took upon himself the curse of humanity to redeem the world. Now risen as Lord, he lays claim to all of life. The reason we're sent out in mission is that all authority has been given to the Son. The world was without God, but now it's claimed in Christ's name.

*

What are the Christian community's meals for? They achieve many things. They express so much of God's grace. They provide a glimpse of what it's like to live under God's reign. They express and reinforce the community that Christ has created through the cross. They're a foretaste of the new creation. They're a great context in which to invite unbelievers so they encounter the reality of God among us. But they're not "for" any of these things. It's a trick question.

Everything else—creation, redemption, mission—is "for" this: that we might eat together in the presence of God. God created the world so we might eat with him. The food we consume, the table around which we sit, and the companions gathered with us have as their end our communion with one another and with God. The Israelites were redeemed to eat with God on the mountain, and we're redeemed for the great messianic banquet that we anticipate when we eat together as a Christian community. We proclaim Christ in mission so that others might hear the invitation to join the feast.

Creation, redemption, and mission all exist so that this meal can take place.

Notes

Introduction: **The Son of Man Came Eating and Drinking**

1. Carolyn Steel, *Hungry City: How Food Shapes Our Lives* (London: Chatto & Windus, 2008), 212.

2. Simon Carey Holt, "Dinner with the Family: A Sacramental Table, Luke 22:7–30" (sermon, Collins Street Baptist Church, Melbourne, August 24, 2008).

3. Nigel Slater, *Toast: The Story of a Boy's Hunger* (New York: Gotham, 2005), 97.

4. John Koenig, *New Testament Hospitality: Partnership with Strangers as Promise and Mission* (Philadelphia: Fortress, 1974), 2.

5. Tim Chester, *Good News to the Poor* (Nottingham, UK: IVP, 2004), 101.

6. Robert J. Karris, *Eating Your Way through Luke's Gospel* (Collegeville, MN: Liturgical Press, 2006), 14.

7. Peter Leithart, *Blessed Are the Hungry: Meditations on the Lord's Supper* (Moscow, ID: Canon Press, 2000), 115.

Chapter 1: **Meals as Enacted Grace**

1. S. Scott Bartchy, "Table Fellowship," *Dictionary of Jesus and the Gospels*, ed. Joel B. Green and Scot McKnight (Downers Grove, IL: InterVarsity Press, 1992), 796.

2. Mary Douglas, "Deciphering a Meal," *Implicit Meanings: Essays in Anthropology* (London: Routledge & Kegan Paul, 1975), 249–75.

3. Ibid., 272.

4. Philip Francis Esler, "Table Fellowship," in *Community and Gospel in Luke-Acts* (Cambridge, UK: Cambridge University Press, 1987), 71–109.

5. Kenneth E. Bailey, *Through Peasant Eyes* (Grand Rapids, MI: Eerdmans, 1980), 90.

6. Bartchy, "Table Fellowship," 796–97.

7. Conrad Gempf, *Mealtime Habits of the Messiah* (Grand Rapids, MI: Zondervan, 2005), 133.

8. Robert J. Karris, *Eating Your Way through Luke's Gospel* (Collegeville, MN: Liturgical Press, 2006), 97.

9. Timothy Keller, *The Prodigal God: Recovering the Heart of the Christian Faith* (New York: Penguin, 2008), 74.

Chapter 2: Meals as Enacted Community

1. Joel E. Green, *The Gospel of Luke, New International Commentary on the New Testament* (Grand Rapids, MI: Eerdmans, 1997), 305, 309.

2. Ibid., 310.

3. Ibid., 309.

4. John Nolland, *Luke 1:9–20*, vol. 35A, *Word Biblical Commentary* (Nashville: Thomas Nelson, 1989), 355.

5. Robert Putman, *Bowling Alone: The Collapse and Revival of American Community* (New York: Simon & Schuster, 2001).

6. Richard Gordon in L. Shannon Jung, *Food for Life: The Spirituality and Ethics of Eating* (Minneapolis: Fortress, 2004), 65.

7. Taylor Clark, *Starbucked: A Double Tall Tale of Caffeine, Commerce, and Culture* (London: Hodder and Stoughton, 2007), 76.

8. Ibid., 78.

9. Ibid., 92.

10. Carolyn Steel, *Hungry City: How Food Shapes Our Lives* (London: Chatto & Windus, 2008), 226.

11. Ibid., 230.

12. Barbara Kingsolver, *Animal, Vegetable, Miracle: One Year of Seasonal Eating* (London: Faber, 2007), 125.

13. Dietrich Bonhoeffer, *Life Together* and *Psalms: Prayerbook of the Bible*, vol. 5, *Dietrich Bonhoeffer Works* (Minneapolis: Fortress, 2005), 36–38.

14. Richard I. Pervo, "Wisdom and Power: Petronius' *Satyricon* and the Social World of Early Christianity," *Anglican Theological Review* 67 (1985): 311.

15. Peter Leithart, *Blessed Are the Hungry: Meditations on the Lord's Supper* (Moscow, ID: Canon Press, 2000), 117.

16. Carolyn Osiek and David L. Balch, *Families in the New Testament World: Households and House Churches* (Louisville, KY: Westminster John Knox Press, 1997), 201–3.

17. Tertullian, *Apology*, ch. 39, vol. 3 of *The Ante-Nicene Fathers: Latin Christianity: Its Founder, Tertullian*, ed. Allan Menzies (Grand Rapids, MI: Eerdmans, 1957), 47.

Chapter 3: Meals as Enacted Hope

1. Cyril of Alexandria, *Homily 48*, New Testament vol. 3, *Ancient Christian Commentary on Scripture: Luke*, ed. Arthur A. Just Jr. (Downers Grove, IL: InterVarsity, 2003), 152.

2. See Robert J. Karris, *Eating Your Way through Luke's Gospel* (Collegeville, MN: Liturgical Press, 2006); and Jerome H. Neyrey, "The Idea of Purity in Mark's

Gospel," in ed. John H. Elliott, *Social-Scientific Criticism of the New Testament and Its Social World, Semeia Studies* 35 (Scholars Press, 1986).

3. Robert Farrar Capon, *The Supper of the Lamb: A Culinary Reflection* (New York: The Modern Library, 1967), 86.

4. Ibid., 85.

5. Eric Schlosser, *Fast Food Nation* (New York: Houghton Mifflin, 2001).

6. Barbara Kingsolver, *Animal, Vegetable, Miracle: One Year of Seasonal Eating* (London: Faber, 2007), 126.

7. Dietrich Bonhoeffer, *Life Together* and *Psalms: Prayerbook of the Bible*, vol. 5, *Dietrich Bonhoeffer Works* (Minneapolis: Fortress, 2005), 73.

8. Cited in Peter Leithart, *Blessed Are the Hungry: Meditations on the Lord's Supper* (Moscow, ID: Canon Press, 2000), 17.

9. Ibid., 18.

10. Carolyn Steel, *Hungry City: How Food Shapes Our Lives* (London: Chatto & Windus, 2008), 14.

11. Andrew Simms, *Tescopoly: How One Shop Came Out on Top and Why It Matters*, (London: Constable and Robinson, 2007), 25, 28.

12. John Piper, *A Hunger for God* (Downers Grove, IL: InterVarsity), 62.

13. Martin Luther in ibid., 185–86.

14. Leithart, *Blessed Are the Hungry*, 20.

Chapter 4: **Meals as Enacted Mission**

1. Craig A. Evans, *Luke, New International Biblical Commentary* (Hendrickson/ Paternoster, 1990), 225.

2. Kenneth E. Bailey, *Through Peasant Eyes* (Grand Rapids, MI: Eerdmans, 1980), 88–113.

3. Joel E. Green, *The Gospel of Luke, New International Commentary on the New Testament* (Grand Rapids, MI: Eerdmans, 1997), 550.

4. S. Scott Bartchy, "Table Fellowship," *Dictionary of Jesus and the Gospels*, eds. Joel B. Green and Scot McKnight (Downers Grove, IL, InterVarsity Press, 1992), 796.

5. Green, *The Gospel of Luke*, 553.

6. Christine D. Pohl, *Making Room: Recovering Hospitality as a Christian Tradition* (Grand Rapids, MI: Eerdmans, 1999), 74.

7. Tim Chester and Steve Timmis, *Total Church* (Wheaton, IL: Crossway, 2008), 80; and Tim Chester, *Good News to the Poor: Sharing the Gospel through Social Involvement* (Nottingham, UK: IVP, 2004), 120–48.

8. Jim Petersen, *Living Proof: Sharing the Gospel Naturally* (Colorado Springs, CO: NavPress, 1989), 119.

9. Philip Yancey, *What's So Amazing about Grace?* (Grand Rapids, MI: Zondervan, 1997), 11.

10. Timothy Keller, *The Prodigal God: Recovering the Heart of the Christian Faith* (New York: Penguin, 2008), 15–16.

11. Carolyn Osiek and David L. Balch, *Families in the New Testament World: Households and House Churches* (Louisville, KY: Westminster John Knox Press, 1997), 194–95.

12. Green, *The Gospel of Luke*, 550.

13. Bartchy, "Table Fellowship," 799.

14. Chester, *Good News to the Poor*, 56–58.

15. John Nolland, *Luke 18:35–24:53*, vol. 35C, *Word Biblical Commentary* (Nashville: Thomas Nelson, 1993), 906.

16. See Keller, *The Prodigal God*, 127–33; and Yancey, *What's So Amazing about Grace*, 19–26.

17. Cited in David Bosch, *Transforming Mission: Paradigm Shifts in Theology of Mission* (Maryknoll, NY: Orbis, 1997), 230.

18. Ibid.

19. Ibid., 232.

20. Simon Carey Holt, "Breakfast on the Beach: An Ordinary Table, John 21:1–14" (sermon, Collins Street Baptist Church, Melbourne, Australia, August 31, 2009).

21. Simon Carey Holt, "Lunch at the Ritz: A Lavish Table, Luke 14:15–24" (sermon, Collins Street Baptist Church, Melbourne, Australia, August 17, 2009).

22. Andrew (Hamo) Hamilton, "Food and Friends Night," *Backyardmissionary* .com (blog), June 14, 2006, www.backyardmissionary.com.

23. Quoted by Drew Goodmanson in a recorded sermon, "Gospel Hospitality: Making Room," Kaleo Church, San Diego, September 2, 2007, www.kaleochurch .com/sermon/gospel-hospitality-making-room.

24. For more on the fear of man, see Edward T. Welch, *When People Are Big and God Is Small* (Phillipsburg, NJ: P&R, 1997).

25. Petersen, *Living Proof*, 119.

26. Ibid.

27. For more on the cost and the cross see Tim Chester, *The Ordinary Hero: Living the Cross and Resurrection* (Nottingham, UK: IVP, 2009), esp. part 2.

28. For more on busyness see Tim Chester, *The Busy Christian's Guide to Busyness* (Nottingham, UK: IVP, 2006), 2008.

29. Jeff Vanderstelt, "Gospel Hospitality in Our Neighbourhood," *Jeff Vanderstelt and Some of His Missional Musings* (blog), April 19, 2009, soma-missionalmusings .blogspot.com.

Chapter 5: **Meals as Enacted Salvation**

1. Peter Leithart, *Blessed Are the Hungry: Meditations on the Lord's Supper* (Moscow, ID: Canon Press, 2000), 11.

2. Ibid., 163.

3. Ibid., 165.

4. Ibid., 164.

5. Wayne A. Meeks, *The First Urban Christians: The Social World of the Apostle Paul* (New Haven, CT: Yale University Press, 1983), 68.

6. Leithart, *Blessed Are the Hungry*, 179–80.

Chapter 6: **Meals as Enacted Promise**

1. David Smith, *Moving towards Emmaus: Hope in a Time of Uncertainty* (London: SPCK, 2007), 4–5.

2. Robert Bringhurst, *A Story as Sharp as a Knife* (Lincoln, NE: University of Nebraska Press, 2000), 47–48.

3. Tim Chester, *The Ordinary Hero: Living the Cross and Resurrection* (Nottingham, UK: IVP, 2009).